Sue Jackson X

D0260705

Prologue to Education

By the same author

Schools of Democracy
(Michigan State University Press)

Prologue to Education

An Enquiry into Ends and Means

John N. Wales

Routledge & Kegan Paul

London, Boston and Henley

To my grandchildren and godchildren

First published in 1979
by Routledge & Kegan Paul Ltd
39 Store Street, London WC1E 7DD,
Broadway House, Newtown Road,
Henley-on-Thames, Oxon RG9 1EN and
9 Park Street, Boston, Mass. 02108, USA
Set in Baskerville 11/12 pt
and printed in Great Britain by
Lowe & Brydone (Printers) Ltd
© John N. Wales 1979

British Library Cataloguing in Publication Data

Wales, John N.

Prologue to education.
1. Education — Philosophy
I. Title
370.1   LB17   78—40887
ISBN 0 7100 0117 7

Contents

Contents

Foreword

by Sir Alec Clegg
formerly Chief Education Officer
West Riding of Yorkshire

Much is written about education, but we seldom find a writer who has taught and who is prepared to scrutinize and at times lucidly to challenge the principles on which current educational practice is based.

John Wales, the writer of this book, has done just this, and he reasons from his own experience. After nearly twenty years of classroom teaching he became involved in making educational films, and in 1948 joined the newly-created Educational Foundation for Visual Aids as Producer. In 1961 he went to UNESCO as adviser on teaching aids and curriculum development in a number of developing countries, and in 1967 became a consultant at UNESCO Headquarters in Paris, where he remained until his retirement.

His concluding chapters in which he looks at educational problems of which we all know, such as co-education, the formal and child-centred education of our Primary Schools, and the traditional and progressive ways of our Secondary Schools, will arouse some criticism and will be challenged. But the real value of what he writes lies in the way he criticizes current principles, values and beliefs, many of which, as he so rightly points out, are based on the conventions and convictions of a previous generation.

He writes from the point of view of a liberal humanist who would almost certainly agree with Carlyle that 'the great law of culture is that each shall become all that he was created capable of being'. It is of the utmost importance at a time when politicians and industry seem determined to bend the educational service to their needs that someone with John Wales' length and breadth of experience should examine the fundamental beliefs on which our education is based. Is the cultivation of individuality in conflict with the need for law and order? Are the current antitheses 'selective' and 'comprehensive', 'traditional' and 'progressive', 'élitist' and 'democratic' valid? Have we sacrificed the education of the spirit to that of the mind? Are we right to identify happiness with good and unhappiness with evil? What place has the cultivation of reason and judgment in our school curriculum when compared with the often sterile transmission of examinable information?

These and a host of other basic questions are thrust by the writer into our disquieted minds, and we need to examine them if we are to avoid being immersed in administrative and political controversy about the education which we currently dispense. We need to examine anew the problems of liberty and equality, the use and abuse of educational convention, the effect on our teaching of convention and coercion, and the prostitution of what should be the promotion of individual growth to current political attempts at social engineering.

These and many other important issues are dealt with by the author who devotes the first half of his book to the ends of education and the second to the means whereby these ends may be attained.

The book should be of major value to those who train teachers and who need from time to time to question the principles which they pass on to their students in training. Indeed it is important to all engaged in education to bear in mind that the full service of primary, secondary and further education is not yet forty years old and is still being fashioned. If as a society we are satisfied with our world as it is, there is reason to continue to do in our schools what we have done in recent decades. If, however, there is much in our society which we find distressing and disturbing, then it is healthy that a man like the writer of this book should ask so basically why we do what we do in our schools and whether what we do is what we need to do.

Preface

This book puts forward, with great diffidence, my own personal profession of faith as a teacher — teaching itself being a profession of faith. In all essentials, the first part was written fifty years ago, at the outset of my career, in an attempt to clarify my own mind; the second, some twelve years later, after I had been teaching for some time. Both parts were laid aside and put on the shelf, as unlikely to be of any general interest or value. Now, when I myself am on the professional shelf at the end of a career which has been, in its various phases, always concerned either directly or indirectly with teaching, and which has taken me, to my great good fortune and enlightenment, to many parts of the world, it has seemed possibly worthwhile to blow the dust off these youthful efforts, in order to see if, in the light of experience, they may be of some wider relevance, and perhaps of interest to other educators, if only as an irritant.

I am the more moved to do this at a time when the whole fabric of the English educational system appears to be in dangerous disarray. Stemming from John Dewey, and nurtured by Marxist philosophy, there has grown up in our time a complacent acceptance of the idea of education being used as a tool of social engineering. That way, as we have seen in other countries, totalitarianism lies; the realization of the concept would mean a complete betrayal of the tradition in which our civilization has developed, the tradition of liberal European humanism with its fundamental insistence on the importance of the individual and, in education, of the drawing out of individual potential. We appear to have got caught up in a net of muddled political philosophy, which confuses 'equality of opportunity' with equality of treatment, not realizing that the two are, in educational experience, mutually incompatible. The results are already apparent in the apotheosis of mediocrity in our schools, and in a meaningless and unnecessary polemical polarization of terms like 'conventional' and 'progressive', 'élite' and 'democratic', 'selective' and 'comprehensive' — an unreal but socially divisive war of words in the waging of which a generation of children — who are only young once — is being sacrificed to the Moloch of political ideology.

I do not know whether it is a reassuring or a disquieting sign that I have found comparatively little to alter after so long a time. There have been some excisions, some amplifications; some things which I have felt it better to express differently, many things I know to be still incompetently expressed. The passage of time and the changes that have taken place in the world of school, as in the world generally, have made some of my thinking out of date. Certain passages, written before the outbreak of the Second World War, I have felt impossible to recast; if they appear wise — or foolish — after the event they were equally wise or foolish before it. But the main themes remain fundamentally unchanged, and where events have overtaken me I take some consolation in the well-known phenomenon that the iconoclast of yesterday becomes the square of tomorrow.

It will be only too obvious that this study owes much to many; I cannot myself tell the measure of my indebtedness to all those living whose writings and conversation have influenced my thinking, and even more to those through the ages whose shades I now salute.

My especial thanks are due to Maruice Ash, Alec Clegg, Kenneth Lindsay and Michael Young for their constructively helpful encouragement, and no less to my daughter Mary Bride Nicholson for her untiring pains in making the draft of this book presentable.

J.N.W.

Ends

Part one

Whatever the world thinks, he who hath not much meditated upon God, the human mind, and the *summum bonum*, may possibly make a thriving earthworm, but will indubitably make a sorry patriot and a sorry statesman.

Bishop Berkeley

My notion of nature comprehends not only the forms which nature produces, but also the nature and internal fabric and organization, as I may call it, of the human mind and imagination . . . .

Sir Joshua Reynolds

God is either Intelligence, or something in its neighbourhood.

Aristotle

So, Socrates, if there are many things about the world — the nature of the divine powers and the origin of the cosmos — of which we cannot give an entirely precise and self-validating explanation, you must not be surprised. Provided the explanation we give is as plausible as any other, we should be satisfied, seeing that I, the speaker, and you, my critics, are only human . . . .

Plato

It is a sottish presumption to disdain and condemn that for false which unto us seemeth to bear no show of likelihood or truth.

Montaigne

The chapters which follow describe a search for an educational ethic. To the professional philosopher they will inevitably seem amateurish; to the professional products of Institutes and Colleges of Education, they may well appear irrelevant or heretical, since they question, either directly or by implication, a good deal of the prevailing educational philosophy of our day. But while I am not for one moment underestimating the contribution of the professional philosopher or the professional educationalist, it is neither of these whom I am primarily addressing; they have their own answers to the problems that I am posing. I am much more concerned with the ordinary parent and practising teacher who are commonly attempting an extremely difficult job without being often at all clear about what they are doing or about their justification for doing it.

Moral attitudes in normal adult life are seldom explicit or systematic; it is part of our inherited cultural tradition that this should be so, part of the fabric of inarticulate taboos with which we are brought up. Moral attitudes in education, on the other hand, normally are fairly explicit and make some attempt to be systematic; parents and teachers are conscious of moral responsibility, and, indeed, find themselves almost compelled in their everyday dealing with children to meet problems of conduct for which they are philosophically ill-equipped.

For what has happened and is still happening is this: in the last seventy years or so the moral code of the ordinary educated man and woman has very considerably changed — changed radically, because the basis of it which was part of a religious tradition has become so weakened by scientific advance and by 'modernist' criticism that it has lost any compelling sanction. The result is that the ordinary man has retained a rather muddled private ethic, a fusion of existing law and convention, traditional doctrine and contemporary fashion, and in practice goes his own way, living morally from hand to mouth and thinking about it as little as possible. Rationalized it usually boils down to a simplified John Stuart Mill liberalism, to the effect that what does not hurt other people is probably all right.

But the same average man as parent or teacher is not happy about anything as negative as this, and, desiring to be on the safe side (rather like the lapsed Christian getting his children baptized), he perpetuates, more or less openly, moral affirmatives in education which are rationally explicable only in terms of a religious tradition and sanction in which he no longer believes, and which his child or pupil will not be expected to believe when grown up. This type of 'morals for the children', rather on the lines of Robert Louis Stevenson's 'religion for the servants', may be more or less intelligently and 'modernistically' done; the variation in practice is wide, from the traditional religious framework of some of the older Public Schools to the undenominational morning assembly now obligatory throughout the state system. From the child's — and from most contemporary adults' — point of view, the difference between School Chapel and School Assembly is unimportant; it is one of degree rather than of kind; the one is as meaningful, or meaningless, as the other. The point for us is that in some form or degree that is the conditioning atmosphere, and that it is intellectually and morally and socially unsatisfactory; inherent in it are hypocrisy and mental slovenliness, and its consequences are to bring the concept of moral values into indifference, ridicule or contempt. Its effects are either to leave the individual with a permanently undergraduate rationalist complacency, or to attract him into a pseudo-religious escapism. When I say pseudo-religious I do not necessarily mean that the religion in question — new or old — is itself spurious; what I mean is that the individual who joins the Catholic Church or the Communist Party or Moral Rearmament or whatever it may be out of a desire for moral security and authority is a pseudo-religious escapist.

I have been talking about the more ordinary and conventional types of education, whether public or private.

4

Modern 'progressive' education does not seem a great deal better off in its ethical theory and practice. Here a reaction from conventional ideas has produced a largely negative attitude. This may at least be intellectually honest – as far as it goes. There is no inculcation of traditional moral or religious beliefs which adults do not hold. How revolutionary this is, and how different from what the ordinary parent expects can be seen from the questions which visitors ask the staff of 'progressive' schools; adults who have themselves long abandoned all religious beliefs and whose morality is of the negative liberal type are genuinely surprised and frequently a little shocked by a school in which there are no religious observances and no direct moral indoctrination.

But apart from a clear gain in intellectual honesty it does not seem that the so-called 'free' school has very much advantage over the conventional; in so far as there is an inarticulate major premiss that a negative attitude on moral questions is desirable it merely produces arid and unintegrated existentialists at school instead of producing them by reaction after school is left. In such an atmosphere, adults who have inherited – and to some extent still retain – positive values tend themselves to become confused; either they hedge by substituting a social for their formerly implicit religious sanction in conduct, using words like 'co-operative' and 'anti-social' instead of 'good' and 'bad', or they find a new ethical code and semi-religious sanction in political idealism of one brand or another. Either alternative begs the whole question of the existence and validity of ethical standards, besides opening the way to an intellectual and moral tyranny, a disguised brainwashing, as vicious as that of any conventional system.

There is, of course, a third possibility which is not uncommon. The honest and self-critical adult who finds no firm ground for standards of behaviour other than that of personal preference may openly adopt this as an ethical outlook. This Utilitarian philosophy has a deceptive simplicity which is very attractive to the young, but its effects are only to put the negative attitude on an intellectually more respectable plane.

Now it surely must be very important to face the issues involved in this whole question of what moral standards are held and taught, and what the justification is for holding and teaching them. Whatever valid criticisms there may be of the traditional Christian religious outlook and its grounds, at least it values were clear-cut and positive; the kind of individual and the kind of society it was likely to produce was, in theory at least, deducible. If we presume to criticize it, we can legitimately do so only on moral grounds which are themselves inherent in the Christian tradition; or on ethical considerations which we feel Christian theory or practice has overlooked or stressed wrongly. It should be possible – indeed, it becomes mandatory – to formulate and expand such a critique into a positive ethic. Any other form of criticism is outside the frame of reference.

But the situation which we at present tolerate – and almost fail to realize or consider – is absurd. The society in which we live, and the educational system which is conditioning the next generation of that society, has lost, save in lip-service, its former allegiance to Christian values, and has no clear idea of any alternative set of values to which allegiance is owed. Nevertheless it is dominated all the time, consciously and unconsciously, by moral terms and attitudes. All this presents direct problems about the kind of individuals we are producing and the kind of society, national and international, which we hope to realize. Few people can be happy about the contemporary world, or look with equanimity on the political, economic and cultural trends which characterize both the developed and the developing countries of our world.

The starting point for any thinking must be to pose the problem in its baldest form. People do habitually think and speak and act in terms of 'ought'; whatever the grounds of moral obligation, a sense of moral obligation is a fact. To lack such sense is exceptional, and those who so lack are designated in our society as either criminal or lunatic. This does not mean that people habitually think and act consciously in accordance with explicit and known moral standards; on the contrary, it is that in all their thinking and action they have a sub-consciousness that a standard is in the background, and in cases of moment, or at conscious appeal, the standard is there to be brought out, like some rather faded, out of date garment, into the crude light of actuality, and if possible made to fit, with a new pattern and a more fashionable cut.

6

We start, then, with the fact of moral consciousness. And at the outset it is well to avoid a possible red herring. Moral consciousness exists both among people for whom the grounds of such consciousness are more or less clearly defined in terms of religious belief, and among those to whom these beliefs are unacceptable or unintelligible. The validity of a religious belief is therefore irrelevant to our discussion, and is productive of much confusion and mental laziness; the religious-minded puts the cart before the horse in a fallacious assumption that there is no sanction or standard for moral conduct apart from the dictates of revealed religion, while the non-religious empties out the baby with the bath-water in a refusal to face clearly the fact and implications of moral consciousness as a problem on its own. A good deal of the confusion in contemporary thinking must be put down to the traditional but irrelevant association of morality with religion. It is manifestly not true that when the religious sanction is absent or removed men cease to act morally. They may cease to interpret aspects and types of behaviour in the same light as the traditional religionist, in the same way that the religionist of one country or century may differ radically from the religionist of another. But religious and non-religious alike continue to think and act in terms of good and bad, and to consider the former desirable and obligatory in conduct and the latter the reverse.

What, then, is this sense of moral obligation that appears to be felt by nearly all adult human beings, independent altogether of belief in a religious sanction, or of the expectation of rewards and punishments in a hypothetical future life? What, if any, are the grounds for such a sense? What problems of practical application — and more especially of educational theory and practice — does it involve? Is any kind of systematic social or individual ethic possible? Finally, in view of the fact that although this sense appears all but universal among adults it is noticeably absent in very young children, how is it acquired, and what kind of moral education can be regarded as desirable and justifiable, and on what grounds? If these questions are academic, they are also highly practical; the whole personal life and psychological development of the individual depends on the things which he thinks right and the things which he in fact does; conflict between these two means loss of energy and direction, and unhappiness both for himself and for those around him. There is thus, quite concretely, a direct relation between morals and morale. And this implies, to some extent at least, the acceptance by society of common standards and the realization of common ethical purposes.

The sense of moral obligation may represent three different things, and its claim to allegiance will differ according to the basis on which it is held:

(a) Right and Wrong, Good and Bad, are merely the reflections and rationalizations of personal preferences or prejudices;

(b) Right and Wrong, Good and Bad, are the reflections and rationalizations of contemporary and traditional social expediencies;

(c) Right and Wrong, Good and Bad, represent metaphysical realities, existing and binding, independent of individual judgment or acceptance, and of social necessity or convenience.

The first proposition is obviously extremely attractive, if only because, by a single negation, it appears to abolish the whole problem. For this reason it is, as I have suggested, the type of explanation around which the progressive school uneasily hovers. If what I think good and right is merely what I personally prefer and advocate, then no moral question enters. Telling the truth, for example, becomes strictly analogous with eating tomatoes; I may do it because I like doing it, but there is no external obligation upon me to do it, and certainly none for anyone who does not share my tastes. One may point out the rational inferences of what in practice would be likely to occur if numbers of people in society behaved capriciously about their aesthetic-moral preferences, but this would merely be to argue in favour of clearsighted and consistent preferences, not to argue against the preference explanation in itself. It is the complete individualist standpoint; the protestant private judgment carried to the ultimate point; the moral anarchism of the heretic denying all authority, save himself. With this, all opinions, all standards, are of subjective, and only subjective, validity.

Attractive at first sight by its simplicity, this explanation soon repels by its transparent shallowness. Chance desires weigh heavy; uncharted freedom tires. Comparatively few mature people will agree that things held to be good or bad are good or bad only for the individual who happens to hold them so; they will agree to differ − or at least agree that differences are conceivable − over details of interpretation, but not over the fact that there is something to interpret. However attenuated any sense of external sanction may have become, a very strong feeling persists that things commonly held to be obligatory are so independent of individual acceptance. Such feeling may be irrational and erroneous; it is often a source of tyranny, as it is also the only real basis of law. But this is not the point; the point is that the feeling exists, and a satisfactory explanation of the nature of the moral sense must take into account this deep and widespread disinclination to accept a theory of moral anarchism.

Next, though it is logically perfectly possible to put all values in preference terms, it is so only by stretching the use of language to an extent which most normal people will find ridiculous. To get drowned, for example, while trying to rescue a complete stranger from drowning may be termed foolhardy or heroic according to opinion, but it is surely inadequate to say that the individual in question performed his action because he wanted to do so. Such an explanation is merely tautologous; it explains nothing. A acts as he does because he is A; his actions affect other people in given ways because they are B, C, D and so on. In a world of unrelated phenomena, in which motives and judgments had nothing in common, such a tautology might conceivably be the only hypothesis that could be achieved. But in fact, in our world, phenomena are not unrelated, and motives and judgments are commonly general. To be satisfactory, therefore, the 'preference' explanation has to explain *why* people prefer certain things as a general norm, and this merely sets the question of the nature of obligation one stage further back − back, ultimately, to the nature of man and of the universe.

The satisfying simplicity of the 'preference' theory is therefore more apparent than real, for while in the third or metaphysical type of explanation the underlying problem is explicitly faced from the start, in this one it is simply shelved.

The second, or social, explanation of the sense of moral obligation is, in our day, probably the one that is most acceptable, and, without any particular consciousness of the fact, the one most commonly held; it fits in with the temper of an age which owes much to the Hegelian-Marxist attitude and analysis, and which is impatient of the older forms of externally imposed doctrine. People may resent being called materialists, but in fact a materialist explanation of any phenomenon is the one first looked-for, and even if it is not found it is normally assumed to be there. Moreover, this social explanation has obviously great truth in it; most of us see little need to look for more complicated explanations when this one is so clearly satisfactory. The values attached in our minds to law and order; the moral penumbra of poverty; the comparative stigma attached to certain types of crime (for example blackmail); the moral sanction behind laws relating to property and inheritance; the emotion of patriotism; the virtues of obedience and conformity traditionally inculcated in education; traditional ideas of sexual morality; social differentiations in certain aspects of the law, for example, gambling and licensing hours; the emotional connotations of the family and the home; popular convictions, however erroneous, regarding the statutory basis of democratic government and the liberty of the individual — all the conglomeration of feelings of Right and Wrong inherent in our social and political life and institutions are quite manifestly explicable in terms of class alignments, of the historical evolution of property relationships, and of political, social and economic development.

And if one traces the significant changes of the past century, and correlates these with alterations in moral outlook, the explanation is still more convincing. A revolution in sex ethics — the permissive society — is following hard upon a revolution in the status of women. Mass production, a vast increase in productivity, and a rapid rise and levelling up of standards of living have led to a complete change of attitude towards work and leisure; industriousness, *per se*, is no longer for us, as it was for our grandfathers, an ethical concept.

Yet, convincing though it is in so many respects, this

explanation is not wholly adequate or satisfactory. It fails to explain two very important things. One is the strength and persistence of a personal moral sense which may, and often does, run counter to the established moral code of a society. Those who attack established institutions and traditional views are commonly the fiercest moralists; their power and effectiveness comes from this. Indeed, it is not unreasonable to suggest that the comparative weakness and ineffectiveness of reformist agitations in our own day compared with those of a hundred or a hundred and fifty years ago are due to the weakness and muddle-headedness of individual moral convictions; if this is true, the inference is obvious, and an additional reason for regarding this discussion as not wholly academic.

Now while in a Hegelian or Marxist sense a revolt against tradition is explicable enough, what is not so easily explicable is the deep sense of personal rectitude which inspires and upholds individuals in unpopular and isolated struggles in which every sanction and every normal emotion and moral bias is against them. That driving force is something more and other than a rationalization of social expediency. In effect, the social explanation accounts for phenomena and their development; it does not account for feelings; it explains why certain values should be inherent in certain societies, not why individuals should strongly attack or support those values. It is a satisfactory pragmatic explanation for the most part, because the mass of people can most easily rationalize their vague and latent feelings of social good and bad — when they are called upon to do so — by arguments of social expediency. But delving deeper, one is again driven back, for any really satisfactory or comprehensive explanation, one stage further — 'why socially expedient?' — if the original feelings are to be accounted for.

Second, this theory ignores what one may call the organic nature of the moral sense. Moral feelings appear to have a snow-ball, or perhaps better, a yeast-like quality; they increase in strength apparently without reason or effort, acquiring a force and sanction unknown to their beginnings. The emotion of national patriotism, for example, and the symbols which evoke it are historically fairly easily explicable; what is interesting for our argument is the enormous

12

psychological power that phrases like 'The Nation', 'The State', 'The People' and the like have grown to possess — power undreamt of in their early manifestations, and one that is now a serious menace to the larger internationalism which is as necessary to the future of civilization now as nationalism was in Europe four centuries ago. Again, the traditional attitude towards incest is historically explicable; what is interesting is the more than rational aversion from the idea felt by people who are bound by no religious sanctions, and who are biologically and anthropologically well-informed. In education, the most trivial matters, like eating spinach or washing before meals, easily acquire a moralistic sanction; for small children the processes of excretion are bound up with a moral vocabulary. This is known to have important psychological consequences, many of them socially harmful in a sense of guilt, conflict, resentment or intolerance that may later appear in wholly other connections; the avoidance of irrationally imposed moral attitudes is one of the chief problems of the Nursery School teacher and the child psychologist. In fact it is exceedingly difficult to get habits acquired that are socially pleasant and convenient without to some extent making a moral business of it, and the 'progressive' Nursery School or Kindergarten, in its desire to avoid being moralistic, often finds itself having to be content with fairly low standards of behaviour.

With the merits and minutiae of all this I am not at the moment concerned; what I am concerned with is to point out that moral values apparently have the quality of spontaneous generation and accretion. The process may also be reversed, though this is probably both slower and less common. An example of this can be seen in dress, and the popular conception of propriety and decency now as compared with half-a-century ago; what used for most Europeans and Americans to be a moral consideration has now almost ceased to be so. So also with blasphemy and obscenity, to neither of which is attached the same moral opprobrium that there used to be, although it has not entirely disappeared. But such changes are largely a matter of fashion, taking now an upward, now a downward curve, rather than of organic evolution; they do not affect the main point, which is that of the general dominance and conditioning power of moral attitudes in individual and social life. Few of us, however intellectually emancipated we may claim to be, can pretend that we are free from some degree of inherited or acquired emotional bias where moral issues are involved. The pacifist is frequently belligerently pacifist; the agnostic is dogmatically agnostic; the materialist holds his philosophy as a matter of faith. How many people can discuss any question of sexual practice or attitude without a certain unscientific self-consciousness or defensiveness? The concept of work is still surrounded with a moral penumbra. I have a wholly irrational feeling of guilt if I read a novel or play cards in the morning, although my hours of work are now entirely my own concern. Idleness or daydreaming is still represented to children as a vice, and the most undiscriminating activity as somehow superior to it — and this by no means only by the traditionally or conventionally minded. Matters of exercise or health are given a moral flavour, and the unenergetic, albeit perfectly healthy, feel on the defensive before the 'brisk walk' or 'cold bath' enthusiasts. Ownership of property carries with it feelings of both right and guilt, and, frequently, attitudes of aggressiveness or defensiveness, patronage or interference, that are socially deplorable. If truth-telling is an obvious social convenience, so also, on occasion, is lying; the latter may even at moments be a moral necessity, and intellectually recognized as such, but nevertheless for most people such moments are occasions of embarrassment and conflict.

The important thing here to recognize is that however the values implicit in all these attitudes originated, and however easily these origins are explicable in terms of social expediencies, all such values have in the process of time acquired a semi-independent existence, and the older they are the less do they correspond with their original nature or social intention, if original nature or social intention there was. Social expediencies may now have little or nothing to do with many popularly held beliefs of right and wrong; in fact, such beliefs are, and in many instances have for some time been, real stumbling-blocks to social and political reform. This is not because of the wickedness of profiteers, the ignorance or stupidity of politicians, the irresponsibility of scientists, or the entrenched selfishness of powerful interests, but because the ordinary average man thinks in terms of 'They' rather

14

than 'I' — i.e., is morally inert and unconsciously in favour of the *status quo*. Revolutions, Communist or Fascist in nature, continue to succeed in the world, not because of potent political philosophy or private lust for power, but because the ordinary average man is uncritical about the use of power in whatever hands, and because the present system of property relationships nationally and internationally throughout the world is grossly unrelated to social and economic needs.

To say, then, that our values are reflections of social expediencies is obviously inadequate. They might conceivably be termed sublimations of original social expediencies; this at least recognizes a psychological process which, while imperfectly understood, is to be regarded as changing and reinforcing original rationalizations with emotional associations and significances. But the mode of expression makes havoc of the original explanation, since one has not begun to explain why the human mind should have this moral-making bias — which is clearly fundamental to the real and original point at issue.

3   Theory and Practice

We are thus inescapably led to the third and most difficult of the attempted explanations, the metaphysical. The word is pretentious in its associations, and I use it — for want of a better — in its most literal sense of something that goes beyond our direct experience and comprehension of physical phenomena.

Now it should be recognized first that a metaphysical explanation is not necessarily the same as a religious one; metaphysics posit something about the ultimate nature of the universe; religion posits one or more divine beings as the ultimate creative principle. The religious explanation, that is to say, is one type of metaphysical explanation.

Second, the particular type of metaphysical explanation anyone may choose to offer to himself or to others is, in the final analysis, unchallengeable, within the limitations of self-consistency. We cannot say that any system of belief is right or wrong; we can only say it is tenable or untenable according to whether it holds together within its own posited terms of reference. But it is worth pointing out at the start that *some kind of choice* of metaphysic seems to be, for the intellectually honest, inescapable, since both of the other possible types of ethical groundwork lead back to some conception of the ultimate nature of things as implicit and as demanding explanation. It cannot be held, therefore, a point against a system of ethical theory that it starts with an unprovable major premise or that it involves a metaphysical hypothesis, if all other systems or denials of system do the same while pretending not to do so. We can demand only of a metaphysical explanation that the premise with which it starts is not disprovable, that this premise is consistent with the verifiable facts of science and experience, and that on it a logically satisfactory superstructure can be built into which

16

the actual problems of conduct in life as we know it — and the resolution of such problems — can be fitted without distortion or contradiction or intellectual legerdemain.

If we go on from this to ask if that — or any other — metaphysical explanation be true, we are stretching words beyond any application of meaning. All we can be justified in saying is that if a metaphysical explanation is, within its own framework of reference, empirically the most satisfactory — or least unsatisfactory — that one can achieve; if it proves a basis for a workable and self-consistent ethic, then it is at least an aspect of truth and to that extent valid. 'All things possible to be believed', said Blake, 'are an Image of Truth.'

And when we say that a metaphysic is even to a partial extent valid, we must be scrupulous to analyse and define what we mean. A theory of moral values based on an outlook on life and on the ultimate nature of things which an individual has thought out to his own satisfaction — at least as a working hypothesis, continually to be revised in the light of reason and experience — such a theory is binding on him, valid in the sense that it is, as it were, his charter, delimiting his rights, his obligations, his liberties as an individual human being in a world of human beings. To be satisfactory, it will have to have much — though not necessarily or by any means everything — in common with similar attempts made by other individuals living in the same society and inheriting the same traditions. A field will be in common, and a field will be his own. Other attempts, made at other times and in different social and historical contexts, will be different again, though there may well be common threads in the fabric.

Ethical validity, then, we conclude, is relative only. This relativity is not the same thing as moral anarchism, the apotheosis of the personal private judgment or whim of taste. The individual can claim that his viewpoint on the universe is necessarily somewhat different from anyone else's; there is, so to speak, a problem of parallax. His viewpoint, being finite, must be to some extent unshared, however slight that extent may be; only a being of infinite faculty would be capable of an apprehension that was a universal Here and Now. But the philosophic outlook that the individual has thought

17

out, and the personal ethic that he derives from this, is not now personal preference or caprice; he is in the position of a constitutional monarch who has signed a Bill of Rights; he has committed himself to a system of law, by which significant generalizations regarding moral behaviour can — indeed must — be made.

Further, the individual is fallible. Even if his philosophy is relatively valid, he may be mistaken in his interpretation of his own law, or he may on occasion break his own law. In other words, he may be wrong or do wrong, and this word has now a content of positive meaning quite other than that of personal dislike. The possibility of error increases as his field of behaviour enters that of others, as in normal social life it does all the time. There is then a complex interaction of interpretations, for the most part, of course, never consciously formulated, and conflict may arise between two or more 'Goods' or 'Rights', or what are apparent to their holders as 'Goods' or 'Rights'. When this happens in any serious degree, each individual is under the moral obligation to think back and see whether the conflict is a real one — i.e. arising from a fundamental difference in original premiss — or, as is far more likely and frequent, only apparent, due to faulty reasoning from a valid original premiss. This is in practice often difficult to realize, because of the heat engendered in moral argument and the emotional overtones that ethical concepts acquire. Nevertheless, the obligation is there. The individual who has no philosophy because he has not troubled to think one out, or who has uncritically taken one over ready-made without realizing its ethical implications, is morally at a disadvantage. Such an individual is, in my view — since his conduct cannot help impinging on others in the society in which he lives — morally as well as institutionally bound by the prevailing code of his community. It is impossible, that is, to be both a moral anarchist and a moral rebel; the rebel must have some standard by which to measure both the object of his rebellion and the motives which make him rebel. If he claims merely to be a law unto himself, he may conceivably be a genius or a criminal or a saint, but socially he is entitled to no more consideration than a rogue elephant.

Ultimate validity is not to be looked for, nor is it necessary. This study would be wildly presumptuous if it were setting out to prove a personal view of the universe to be correct; all it can legitimately attempt to do is to suggest that *some* personal view is necessary if a man is to live with himself and with his fellows.

Yet if one is not to remain entirely within the realm of myth or fantasy, one has to acknowledge that with even the most tentative and diffident philosophy there must be something more to it than a personal projection, a home-made working model. My world is other people's; we share the same life; respond to the same stimuli; strive for the same bread and butter; undergo the same emotional storms of love or anger. However significant a reservation we make regarding the individual life, the unique consciousness and angle of vision, we have to agree that the life we have in common with other people is for most of us at least as important as the life we have on our own. Even our thoughts are interactions; they are not spontaneously generated, and their effects go on like ripples on a pond long after the stone has sunk. If in fact the things I feel possible to believe are images of truth — even distorted images, shadows in the cave — that gives my judgments of right and wrong *some* practical importance; I must not be categorical or dogmatic about them, but I must be prepared to say on occasion not only that I may be wrong but that other people may be wrong also and that in my reasoned opinion they are. Further, being in the world I must act on my opinion; as a citizen, my actions or my lack of action must equally affect the community.

This whole discussion started off with a fundamental datum. This was that moral consciousness is a fact of our existence. We have to accept as no less fundamental the fact of social environment. No outlook can be scientifically and intellectually satisfactory that premises the individual *in vacuo*. Fundamental considerations apart, the individualist 'preference' explanation in ethical theory is untenable in practice because in practice all opinion is reflected in social action which again has repercussions in social opinion, and so on indefinitely. I cannot avoid impinging upon, and being affected by the actions of others; I cannot avoid swaying or being swayed by their views. This is a matter of common experience which is integral to all ethical discussion. Personally held moral opinions, if they are at all strongly held —

19

and they almost always are strongly held — are inevitably the object of either hostility or concurrence; in either case they are likely to be reinforced. We lay down the law for others even in spite of ourselves, if not in action, then at least by approval or disapproval which we cannot conceal. For educators this is a fundamental problem.

All this being so, any initial premiss has to include and accept the fact of society. We may regard it as a good to be fostered and supported, or as an ill to be avoided as far as possible. But we cannot ignore it. If we accept it as at least a comparative good, which means if we continue to live with and have more or less stable relationships with our fellows in society, rather than commit suicide or become economically self-sufficient hermits, then automatically we enter the region of moral obligation, if only because in society as we know it feelings of moral obligation exist among and condition the behaviour of its members. Or, more precisely, we enter the region of moral obligation conceived as a common principle, and not merely as a personal projection. Good and Bad are already defined for us — not sharply, perhaps, nor very coherently, but recognizably compulsive — by centuries of social experience and of symbolic associations. And the initial fact of entry into, acceptance of and acceptance by society makes this existing code binding on the individual — unless (and this is a point of the first importance) the individual can assert a higher ethic which he can claim the contemporary social ethic transgresses or fails to take into account.

Now all this implies a great deal, and begs certain questions. It implies that Reason is a fact, and also that it is a Good. It suggests, further, that people in society do hold ethical views in common, and agree, at least on fundamentals, more than they disagree. Both these assumptions, if true, are very important to our discussion.

Both are true, at least to a very considerable extent, as matters of common experience, and we need not claim for them at this stage any further validity. Despite the present state of the world, and the frequently devastating irrational behaviour of individuals and groups, it is nevertheless a fact that people in their ordinary lives, when not swayed by emotional stress, do implicitly and explicitly appeal to Reason in nearly every action and every speech they make. So habitual is this — for all social intercourse, books, education, commerce, speech itself, pivots on it — that few even stop to consider rationality as debatable; its absence would mean unrecognizable chaos. There may be and is legitimate doubt about the place of Reason in a hierarchy of values, but that it is, pragmatically at least, a value of some kind is extraordinarily difficult to doubt.

And that there is a 'common-sense' of mankind, or rather of a given group of men at a given time, is common experience also. It may not be infallible or consistent, and it may change from time to time and from place to place; it is obviously conditioned by special factors, such as war, pestilence, sudden disaster, economic stringency, and equally by long untroubled interludes of peace and prosperity, and a high level of achievement in the arts and sciences. But such changes and fluctuations in the *mores* of a society are not arguments against there being, at any given moment, some sense of common values to which general importance is attached: which, in fact, is generally enforced or morally imposed by a more or less defined code of law and convention. The validity of this code is the degree of common acceptance which maintains it; laws and conventions which cease to command common respect rapidly lose their sanction and become obsolete.

What men in general believe to be good is at least good for them at their moment of conviction; we are really saying no more than that, and put in this form it is little more than a tautology. What we have to go on to ask, in this empirical preface, is whether there is discoverable in the moral sense and ideology of mankind any considerable uniformity or continuity over a wide range of human experience. If in fact there are things in which people believe, and to which they attach moral importance over long periods and with few exceptions; more important still, if there appears to be a discernible principle of development in the nature and intensity of such beliefs, then here would be a side-light at least on the nature of the universe as human beings see it and experience it, and a rough empirical check on any ethic that a

21

personal metaphysic may independently reach and adhere to. The next step must be, then, to consider whether there are any substantial grounds for such an approach.

At this stage it may be serviceable to consider, at least in a rather broad and elementary way, what qualities human beings appear reasonably united in approving, and in what respects and to what degree emphasis of approval has in fact shifted within periods of human experience about which we have relevant documentary record.

Reason we have already suggested as one such quality, never, perhaps, rated very high as a virtue, and, save in certain epochs, approved implicitly, rather than explicitly. More admired but less respected is a kindred but rather vaguer quality, Understanding. This includes both a deliberate intellectual process of ordered knowledge based on direct sensory perception or on inference from observed phenomena, and an intuitive process which may be instinctive and may even involve what has come to be called extra-sensory perception. In its fullest sense it seems to imply some degree of emotional fusion with the object, as well as intellectual grasp of it. It is doubtful if the real mental processes which we thus consciously and unconsciously demarcate are as compartmented as our names for them suggest; it is a continual danger and pitfall that in our thought-forms we tend to become intoxicated by the convenient label.

Reason, then, and Understanding. Closely allied with both of these is Judgment, the quality, difficult to define, of accurate assessment, of knowing and hitting the mark, more overt than Understanding, more inclusive than Reason, but combining something of both. Integrity, a compound quality at once more realistic and more ruthless than Honour, more intelligent than Innocence, both of which conceptions it includes. Courage, of whatever kind, and almost for whatever motive; Charity, in its older religious connotation, meaning the capacity for loving-kindness and tolerance, comprehension

23

and compassion, but without weakness or sentimentality. Both Strength and Humility, both often in practice liable to abuse or to spurious manifestations. And last, Order in both personal and public life, a certain seemliness and shapeliness in patterns of behaviour and in social institutions, a reticent avoidance of flamboyance or excess or hysterical demonstration, a respect for law, custom and tradition, the antithesis equally of both anarchy and tyranny.

This is not a presumptuous attempt to re-write the Ten Commandments or the Seven Cardinal Virtues; these may be individual imperatives, with sanctions of their own. What I am concerned to suggest is something far more pragmatic. It seems to me that with certain differences from time to time in relative emphasis, and with certain significant additions or omissions in particular societies in particular epochs, the list I have outlined above has been and remains the accepted moral code approved by civilized man in every culture within our knowledge. Egypt, China, Greece, Rome, Byzantium; Mongolia under Kablai Khan, India under Akbar, Mexico under Montezuma; Christian Europe from Charlemagne to our own day; the precepts of Lao-Tse, the analects of Confucius, the teachings of Buddha, Christ, Mahomet: the values that all these have in common are significantly similar.

And the omissions in our list; those things which some societies have held as values, and others as unimportant, are either part of a specific religious tradition − e.g. Piety, Chastity, Respect for Parents − or are economic or climatic in their origin and application − e.g. Temperance and Diligence. Few of these are universal enough, nor sufficiently permanent in the way they are interpreted, to serve our purpose: moreover, they are secondary rather than primary in importance, belonging to the superstructure rather than the foundations of conduct.

But the list we have, if it is at all accurate, is significant and impressive. Here we have a fair picture of man's better nature as he sees it in many very different parts of the world and in many very different social contexts. However mankind may have been divided by historical circumstance, geographical conditions, economic limitations, political institutions and religious beliefs, it appears to be united, however unconsciously, in a common approval of the qualities of Reason,

Understanding, Judgment, Integrity, Courage, Charity, Strength, Humility, Order.

It is an interesting commentary, this, on the bloodthirsty records of human history; the tale of cruelty, irrationality, greed, murder, bigotry and treachery that the history books present. Yet what is most interesting about it is that men seldom believe themselves to be bloodthirsty, bigoted or treacherous. Milton's Satan may cry 'Evil, be thou my Good'; human beings seldom do. Normally men act, and if we are to believe their own accounts have throughout history always acted, from the highest motives. Wars are almost invariably undertaken to restore order, to rescue people from tyranny, to spread the blessings of civilization. Treachery is explained as a desire to save bloodshed and destruction, by speeding up the acceptance of inevitable defeat. Religious bigotry and cruelty, interpreted *sub specie aeternitatis*, become enlightened kindness, saving immortal souls at the trivial cost of temporal bodies.

There is a further point here. If this contradiction could be dismissed as mere hypocrisy, it would not be a matter for serious comment; hypocrisy, after all, has been defined as the tribute that vice pays to virtue. The interesting and important thing is why men think it necessary to pay this tribute; it implies an acceptance of virtue as a norm to be approved even when in practice vice prevails. The real problem arises not from the fact that men are hypocritical, but that they are fundamentally sincere; they believe themselves, and desire others to believe them, to be moral beings acting morally; if they commit actions that appear to others revolting and intolerable, such actions are never admitted as naked sadism or self-interest; they are justified and explained on some unimpeachable moral ground. The mass genocide of Jews, the discrimination against Negroes, the sporadic wars between variant Christian faiths, the internecine massacres of and by Hindus and Muslims, even the horrors of Hiroshima and Nagasaki, have all found their sincere moral defenders.

And what we can notice further is that, however despairing we may well feel inclined to be about the state and future of the world of increasingly militant nationalism and racism, nevertheless, in spite of all the violence and irrationality, the trend of history, in terms of the values on our list, has been up rather than down. The growth of science and technology, while providing the weapons of destruction, has enormously increased the scope of rational thought and activity in everyday life. The growth of psychological knowledge has widened our understanding, and has suggested the possibility of a process of direct perception; education and the rise of material standards of living have contributed to the increase of personal dignity and integrity — small enough, it is true, over the world as a whole, but perceptible even in developing countries, and fairly definite if we compare the common man in Western Europe or North America today with his ancestor as portrayed in diaries, novels and popular drama two or three centuries ago. Cunning is less admired; Odysseus of the many wiles is not quite the heroic figure he was. The concept of Courage has widened; a Father Damien and an Edith Cavell can take their place among the heroes, and beside them the horse-play of the Crusades and the stagy heroics of Fontenoy or Balaclava appear a little grotesque. Kindness and Tolerance have, historically, increased out of all knowledge; the narrow tyranny of parents towards their children or of husbands towards their wives which was an historical commonplace only a little while ago has been largely eroded. While our knowledge of and sympathy with mental illness remains limited, we no longer take pleasure in mocking or punishing insanity, and our treatment of juvenile crime or sexual aberration is at least comparatively enlightened. So much has tolerance increased that when faced with organized and systematic violence we are somewhat at a loss. The reason why the Hitler régime was allowed to take such strong hold was very largely because ordinary people throughout the world, and even in Germany itself, just could not believe their eyes and ears; it was impossible for such atrocities to be true. The same was so with the Stalinist régime in Russia. Today, we feel the same paralysis of will, of not knowing what attitude or action to take, when we are faced with race riots in the USA or in England, with organized racial discrimination in South Africa or with apparently senseless terrorism in Northern Ireland. We find it hard to credit deliberate and officially inspired brutality on the part of the supposed guardians of law and order, or officially calculated and fostered mob violence, or legal trials that are official travesties of justice. All these things happen, all over the world, in greater or lesser degree. But they are so alien to the value-system that our society has come to take for granted that we tend to regard them as some sort of nightmare from which we shall presently wake up.

There is a great danger here; our very moral sense may be our undoing. Unless we can change ourselves and our social institutions quickly enough to remove the conditions which give certain individuals and groups the power and motive to act criminally; unless too we can redress the balance now existing which gives the destructive potentialities of science and technology priority over the constructive; then we may at any moment be faced with a crisis in which the whole civilizing process may be turned back into a chaos which we have not developed the intelligence to prevent and have lost the ruthlessness to resist. It would be an ironical ending to many aeons of conscious and unconscious endeavour, but it is doubtful if the human race would survive to be amused, nor would the Juggernaut of cause and effect pause to point the moral.

Strength and Humility have both declined as popular virtues; personal strength is obviously of diminished practical importance in a machine civilization; humility is hard to sustain with sincerity in a generation that is technologically omni-competent and theologically self-sufficient. Judgment — the 'not-too-much' of the Greeks and Romans, the 'middle-way' of Buddhists and others — has never ranked in theory as high in the West as in the East, though in practice a rather muddled genius for illogical compromise has proved a sort of substitute. But there can be little doubt that this quality has, in the world generally, increased; the influence of scientific method and the growth of legal practice and codification have given it prestige; technical and economic developments have done the same, attaching an increased value to precision, and to co-ordination of hand, eye and brain. Aesthetic judgment has probably not increased qualitatively; quantitatively the basis of its exercise has, with education, mass-communication and the democratization of the arts, broadened very greatly. Order in personal life would seem to have gained; people's lives are in general less messy, chaotic and rudderless, less 'nasty, brutish and short' than they were. In public

27

life possibly the reverse is true; two world wars, a depressing number of totalitarian régimes, and a general decline in the quality of parliamentary government, have lowered our tolerance of law enforcement; we conform — possibly too much — but we have little respect of liking for conformity; there is a substantial amount of non-conformity too.

Such, in the large, and for what they are worth, would appear to be the main facts about the moral consciousness of man in society, and such to be the directions in which that consciousness has been mainly evolving. Here and there individuals — Jesus Christ and the Buddha are examples — stand out who defy that code, setting in its place an ethic wholly different. Such individuals appear extremely rare in history. More commonly, as with a Machiavelli or Nietzsche, particular accepted virtues or values are stressed at the expense of others, to point a lesson peculiar to a given time or place. More commonly still, individual criticism is directed not so much at the values that are commonly accepted, as at the inadequate or hypocritical or inconsistent or out-dated interpretation of them in current practice. Such criticism is the theme of most of the great religious books, and of most satire; the Old and New Testaments and for example the Koran on the one hand, Erasmus, Voltaire, Shaw and Orwell on the other, have motives and values in common, however much they may differ in modes of expression or in techniques of reform.

Historically, again, there occur, or apparently occur, periods in which the upward trend is reversed, periods which give the lie to the concept of an evolving moral consciousness. It is possible that our own time is such a period. It is fatally easy to prove anything from history, and examples picked to support a thesis prove nothing either way. Even if a trend is discernible, there is no reason to suppose that the curve is a steady one, nor, indeed, that it may not at any time be reversed. But however tentative we may be, and with whatever reservations we may hedge our conclusions, such objective evidence as we can gather seems to point to the existence of a moral 'common-sense' in civilized man, and to that sense becoming more consciously and more discriminatingly cultivated. Any metaphysic we may attempt must square with this empiric evidence, must relate it to other facts of science and experience, and seek to interpret the whole complex in terms of a universal process.

5   Validity and Truth

An entirely mechanistic conception of the universe such as was attempted by the post-Darwinists appears to be no longer adequate, and to have been generally abandoned. And, save by fundamentalists of the Jewish, Christian or Islamic faiths, the opposite hypothesis of external, intermittent and arbitrary interventions by an omnipotent Providence appears equally untenable. Thanks to this general retreat from the picturesque simplicities of legend there is popularly but erroneously supposed to have been a reconciliation of science and religion. In fact what has been established is a concordat. Now that the first fears, arrogances and confusions have diminished, religion and science have settled down to cultivate agreed, and mutually almost exclusive, spheres of influence. The hysterical pulpit thunder of Wilberforce against Darwin strikes rather thin and cracked upon the modern ear; nowadays those who choose to start with the required initial premiss can claim for their ancestors a spiritual home in Paradise, and still acknowledge without embarrassment their biological relations in the Zoological Gardens. One of the few clear gains of the last hundred years is that such problems no longer worry us.

Further, the use of such words as material and non-material, organic and inorganic, subjective and objective, has become largely illusory. Matter is no longer a static thing, conceptually unrelated to life or mind; Planck, Rutherford and Einstein have demolished the minutely small billiard ball that our grandfathers pictured as the atom, and the infinitely large envelope that they pictured as unversal space. We genuinely do know a great deal more about these fundamental facts of physical science than mankind has ever known before; this is not just a change in fashion, in modes of thinking; the facts that have been revealed by the spectrograph, the cloud-

30

chamber, the electron microscope, X-ray crystallography, the interferometer and the radio-telescope — to mention only a few of man's modern windows on the universe — must be accepted as basic by anyone who has not committed himself to a philosophy that holds all phenomena to be illusion. Not only has the physicist come to know a great deal about the nature of the universe and the ultimate structure of matter; with the discovery of the DNA double helix the biochemist has come very near knowing the ultimate structure of life. Both are now in the doubtfully happy position of being able to synthesize their materials into compounds indistinguishable from those produced by nature, and even into such that nature never achieved. The alchemist is no longer a figure of legend, engaged upon an impossible and sacrilegious quest; he has become much more like a boy with a 'Do-It-Yourself' kit. This revolution, with all that it entails to our patterns of thought and behaviour, has occurred in my lifetime.

The universe with which contemporary science presents us is not one of things, but of dynamic relationships, and if we ask 'Relationships between what?', we find that both question and answer can finally be put only in terms of mathematical symbols. All else is analogy, useful and even essential for the layman's comprehension, but limited in application, inadequate, and liable to mislead. Nature, on final analysis to date, consists of processes and predispositions.

If first causes remain unknown, and possibly unknowable, we can say with some certainty that from elemental forces, and in conditions which we can only hazard, have developed by increasing complexity of structure and diversity of powers what we call Matter and what we call Life. And we must in logic add to this development process the emergence of such attributes of Matter and Life as what we know as Mind and, for human beings at least, Personality. In this development process two principles appear to stand out. Each successive creation, as we go up the scale in both the inorganic and the organic worlds, possesses potentialities for future creativeness which were not discernible in their origins. Second, each phenomenon is not an entity in itself, isolated and self-contained, but an event in a space-time continuum, with a surrounding field of functions and powers interacting with others in space and in time. Whether we call this development process 'creative' or 'emergent' is immaterial; the point for us would seem to be that the direction in which development has taken place is inherent, a fundamental bias in the nature of things.

In the physical and biological sciences, analytical methods and static conceptions remain useful, and within limits valid, for the purpose of isolating and studying phenomena, even when it is realized that ultimately no phenomenon is isolated. But when thought attempts to express in words processes of which thought itself is a development and a rudimentary expression — when, that is, we are dealing with mental phenomena, and attempting to analyse and systematize our own experience and our own ideas of things of which we can have only a second-hand and subjective realization — then 'logic coils round itself and bites its own tail'. When philosophers deal with ideas as abstractions, they are ultimately measuring things in terms of themselves, since they cannot get outside their conceptual experimentation in the way that chemists, physicists and biologists are, to a great extent at least, able to do. Whatever the real nature of things, our experience of them is not isolatable, and is of necessity indirect and circumstantial. Ideas do not come to our examination as fresh laboratory specimens; they are already part of our mental fabric; they are already inseparable from other ideas, and from their own past histories; each part of our experience is a complex process in several dimensions. Concepts reach and impinge on our thinking already stale with the accretions of former thought and experience, overgrown with the results and interactions of other concepts in other minds; each is experienced and interpreted by us in the context of our existing experience, our existing mental equipment and predisposition; we experience and interpret it extensively in time and space, intensively in degree and quality of apprehension. The result is that words like God, Man, Spirit, Life, Mind, Survival, Truth, Goodness, Beauty and many more come to us already overloaded with meaning, and around the spark of reality for which such words are symbols there is for each one of us a sort of personal and subjective penumbra which conditions and thwarts our scientific intentions.

32

So when we come to the idea of evolution in the mental and moral worlds we are faced with immense and inescapable difficulties. Yet before we leave science for speculation, we must admit that some evolution must have taken place. Whatever reservations we may and must make about the limited validity of the analytical approach in dealing with philosophical concepts, we are at least justified in claiming for the development of the human being as objective and factual a reality as for any other natural phenomenon. Man, the creature infinite in faculty, the creature with immortal longings, has, as a matter of biological fact, developed. Whatever these words mean, they do mean something which human beings recognize and respond to, and this recognition and response are themselves scientific phenomena to be explained. Even if they mean nothing, and man's conception of himself is a gigantic piece of subjective self-deception, then still we have to account for such an hallucination coming into existence. For here 'subjective' and 'objective' lose whatever meaning they ever had; a universal human error must be for human beings a universal truth.

If, therefore, what we know as Life was the first great mutation in our history, what we know as Mind must have been the second. If this tendency to make structures at once more complete and more potentially creative resulted, among other things, in Man as a biological organism, it must also have resulted in Mind as a biological force. Mind would not have survived if its first manifestations had run counter to the evolutionary stream, would not have evolved if it had not been integral with the evolutionary process. We cannot scientifically or philosophically regard Mind as a thing apart, a full-grown control externally imposed; it can only have grown up with the organisms that possessed it or possessed the potentiality for it. It is as difficult to say where Mind begins as where Life begins, nor is it essential that we should be able to do so. The point is that consciousness in some form or other, at one level or another, is in the direct line of evolutionary succession; it is yet another successful experiment in relation-making, along a line of direction that is already well-marked.

There is no need to be teleological about this, to read into this process an *Anima Dei* or an *Anima Mundi*; we have not yet got to the point where such a concept need be considered. We are still dealing with scientific phenomena, and first causes or final purposes are irrelevant; our argument must stand independent of them.

But in the creative force of Mind we are dealing with something new, something unknown before. With the accession of consciousness the organism's field of effective relationship with its environment was clearly considerably extended. With the accession of reflective reason, the capacity for conscious choice and conscious self-direction, it is extended out of all recognition. A process is enormously accelerated when it becomes deliberate. Even a fairly obtuse individual can, with a little concentration, learn to perform an unaccustomed action quite quickly; having learnt the principle of it, he can apply his new-found skill without difficulty in other conditions. He can, indeed, by thought, if not add a cubit to his stature, at least increase, by deliberate practice, either his mental or his physical powers to a considerable extent. It is, of course, also true that he can reverse the process; organisms can and do degenerate; abilities can rust; both bodies and minds can get soft and flabby. Nevertheless it can hardly be questioned that man's ruling position in the animal creation is due to his development of conscious reflective reason as a driving force, giving him a greater independence and a greater control of his environment.

And in all this the development of Mind as reflective reason is only part of the story. The creative power of the imagination has been part of man's development also. This is true not only of the human capacity to create works of art which awaken creative responses in other minds, though such stimulus and response is also a field of psychological study. But even more significant for our argument is the effect on, the partial control of, the physical body which the creative imagination undoubtedly possesses. Leaving out such extreme cases as the production, well-authenticated in the history of religious mysticism, of physical stigmata, we need for this only instance recent medical research in the field of the hormones and the glands of internal secretion, or in what have come to be called psychosomatic disorders. Here we have nervous stimuli responding to mental stimuli, and reacting directly to produce symptoms of physical disease. Men and women can, and very frequently do, think themselves into being really ill; equally, they can think themselves into being well. Even such common human frailties as worry or bad temper we know now to be physically toxic, physiologically destructive to the organism.

Of the full extent and importance of all this we as yet know comparatively little; psychology and psychological medicine are still sciences only in embryo, and our knowledge of the structure of the mind is nothing comparable with our knowledge of the structure of the atom or of the living cell. But it is sufficient for our immediate purpose to recognize that the manifestations and powers of mind fall coherently and explicably into the general pattern of development that we have already noted. In accordance with what would appear to be a generally persistent creative process, the components which combined to result in the development of the human being produced a more than mechanical unit, a sum of its parts; they produced a unit which was at the same time a field of manifold functions and forces, with a capacity for further creativeness which could not be gauged from a mere aggregation of components, the whole coming to be dominated by a semi-independent control which was itself an earlier product of the same developing process.

But if Mind has emerged as a potentially creative force, what are we to say of the conceptions, the creations, of Mind? If original expediencies and necessities have been dignified through its creative transmutation into values, have these not, in logic, a real, as well as a relative, validity? If this universal tendency to make new structures has worked out so far, and Mind is at one and the same time its product and its abettor, then the ideas which Mind has evolved to express to itself alignment with and departure from this tendency must also be assumed to acquire the character of creative semi-independent forces. The Platonic 'Idea' does not, on our analysis, appear mere metaphysical fantasy.

We are now out of the realm of science, and in that of speculation. We started with both feet firmly on the ground; we are now only on tip-toe — 'stretching out hands in longing towards a further shore'. Are absolute values and ideas the apotheosis of survival values and ideas? That is the suggestion;

let us, at the risk of repetition, summarize our thesis so far, and see how it stands.

There is, we have argued, in the nature of things a certain orientation, a bias on the wheel. Bergson called it 'creative', Lloyd Morgan 'emergent', Smuts 'holistic'; the label is not important. The point is that, for all phenomena, the state of being is also the state of becoming. All things are in a state of more or less unstable equilibrium, oscillating, as it were, with a certain inherent disposition, a tendency which is in general one towards making more complex and more independent structures. In these structures, the components, by combining, not merely mixing, acquire collectively an element of newness and an increase of potential. In this process the advent of, first, Life, and then, Mind, were important landmarks, giving it, by conscious direction, an enormous acceleration. This direction has now become partially external. The Mind, being itself a whole within a whole, has a world of its own; its control pervades every part of the organism, yet it has the power of putting itself partially outside the organism. We are, as individuals, mentally as well as physically, the heirs of all the ages, and only through the difficult commerce of mind with mind can this heritage be still further enriched. None of us can think, speak, write or even feel without expressing our debt to people living and dead; we can take no step that is not in praise or dispraise of famous men.

This realm of thought, of which our consciousness of moral values is an integral part, has grown as have all other structures; if we consider it apart, we do so with our eyes open, and for convenience only. A whole within a whole, a field cutting across other fields, it is, most illusive of all, measurable only in terms of itself. Nevertheless we are, and must be, the measure of all things, and it has not been through too humble a sense of our limitations that we have made our progress from the slime. Indeed, following our earlier reasoning, we must see that this freedom which the mind enjoys is but another facet of that tendency which has resulted, among other developments, in human personality. The more complex a structure is, the more independent it is, as well as more interdependent; the two qualities are correlative, not contradictory.

Mind as we know it is a late-comer on the earth; its life is measured in thousands of years while the history of the physical world is measured in millions. From unconscious gropings it has become the control that we know. In its earlier stages the course shaped it; in its later it has helped to shape the course. This is not to exaggerate its importance. The course is the course of the universe, in which we are a parvenu and possibly ephemeral creation. If we can conceive such a concerted act of hubris on the part of mankind as a deliberate attempt to reverse the course — a Third World War, for example, fought with nuclear weapons — mankind could deservedly vanish, but the blind game of trial and error would go on as before. Up till now, human arrogance and perversity have been exceeded, on balance, by more constructive human qualities, both mental and moral; at any rate, history has shown, in spite of all its black pages, an upward rather than a downward trend; mind has gone with the stream and added impetus to it, as the reign of the human race bears witness. 'In the country of the blind, the one-eyed man is king'; in the structural universe, the least disorderly creation will be the most powerful. But this gives no grounds for human complacency. Man is a constitutional monarch existing on a conditioning charter; he reigns only as long as he obeys the law.

We have depicted the universe as structural, orderly and creative. But we should continue to avoid the confusion of mind which would, on this slender evidence, plunge into teleology. The structural and creative tendencies come from within, not from without; they are in the nature of things. To postulate a pre-existing and perfect Universal Mind directing a course which began in chaos, and in which for millions of years no mind as we conceive it was perceptible, is surely to put the cart before the horse in a manner only possible to those in whom intelligence is not permitted to temper dogma.

The question of religion is in a sense a side-issue, not essential to the main thread of our argument, and liable even to confuse it. Yet, in a study which professes to be relevant to Education, it seems cowardly to evade it; a background of religious belief looms heavily in nearly all educational systems — even in countries where education is officially secular — and this background conditions the patterns of thought and behaviour of teacher, parent and child.

Religion is, after all, one of the first fruits of the conscious mind; it is an attempt to explain the inexplicable. The savage, whose economy is at the mercy of apparently capricious elements, fears the gods whom he conceives as controlling, or identifiable with, these elements, and tries to insure his fields and flocks by sacrifice; among primitive peoples, and peoples by no means primitive, the priest, the god-persuader, is king, and social laws grow up under divine sanction, which add to them considerable potency. If modern so-called civilized man finds himself crying

> I, a stranger and afraid,
> In a world I never made,

it is small wonder that his forefathers should have feared and tried to propitiate what they did not understand.

And we, who have all this in our blood, and much else besides, what are we to say? The haunting uncertainty remains.

> The present life of man upon earth, O King [said the thegn at Edwin's court] seems to me, in comparison with that time which is unknown to us, like the swift flight of a sparrow through the house, wherein you sit at supper in winter, with your ealdormen and thegns, while the fire blazes

in the midst and the hall is warmed, but the wintry storms of rain and snow are raging abroad. The sparrow, flying in at one door and out immediately at another, whilst he is within he is safe from the wintry tempest; but after a short space of fair weather, he immediately vanishes out of your sight, passing from winter into winter again. So the life of man appears for a little while, but of what is to follow or what went before we know nothing at all. If, therefore, this new doctrine tells us something more certain, it seems justly to deserve to be followed.

But, alas, this is just what no doctrine can do, new or old; to this age-long cry for certainty, the answer is always and inevitably a dusty one.

To hark back. We hazarded that the entity which we call Mind was at one and the same time a member of two different larger entities; that there was, so to speak, to some extent a divided allegiance. First, it was closely bound up with the physical organism in the comparatively small domain of personality; second, in its faculty for making concepts, ideas and abstractions which had, snowball-like, an increasing weight upon succeeding generations of men, it was bound up in another and much larger domain, which we called the realm of thought. Here ideas might begin to have the reality which Plato claimed for them; and here might perhaps be found the logical justification for our values which men of science have pronounced impossible, and men of faith unnecessary. Here ideas become ideals, Truth, Beauty, Goodness and the rest become beacons of spiritual reality; morality becomes infused with a sanctioning emotion. 'The poet sings, "Dear City of Cecrops"; why may not I say, "Dear City of God"?' This larger citizenship, whose splendid vision has attended poets and painters, saints and seers, all 'god-intoxicated' men, is no cold abstraction of the concept-making mind; something more, some intenser quality has entered in.

Some intenser quality. But has not the whole process as we have envisaged it been an increasing realization of this? More complex structures; more subordinate and coordinate functions; the entity more independent and in increasing control of its environment; more varied and richer potentialities of experience; consciousness, feeling, and power of deliberate choice entering in to give impetus and acceleration to the process.

The human being is, as far as we can tell, at once the most free and the most intensely conscious phenomenon in nature; reason and imagination have discovered for mankind a new world of joys and terrors which, for the rest of the animal creation is apparently very dim, if not unknown. And human beings differ among themselves according to age, experience, and individual personality. Children are notoriously animal, and those who cling to the delusion of the superior vision or the superior virtue of childhood find little basis for their Rousseauism in the normal hard-headed and self-seeking child. This is not a criticism of children; to be self-seeking, in its most literal sense, is an essential quality for a developing personality needing to apprehend and realize its powers. But the quality of perceptivity and sensitivity which the developing human being acquires in greater or lesser degree is an essential one to his mental and moral growth, and to the establishment of full and stable relationships with his environment. Appreciation of this quality is reflected in our everyday values; the phlegmatic man has not the same place in our regard as the man of feeling; magnanimity ranks higher than the nicely calculated less or more; the artist, who sees 'not with, but through, the eye', adds to the vision of us all.

Ideals, then, are no more foreign to our nature than ideas. The realm of the Mind has, on the borders of its expanding territory, a still less charted region, the domain of the Spirit.

Matter to Life, Life to Mind, Mind to Spirit. If all this is true — true in the sense of satisfying the criteria of logic and experience that we laid down for ourselves — here is religion enough. It seems to me a concept of creation far more satisfactory than that of a fall from an original perfection, to see ourselves as travelling along a road which others have travelled before, a road in process of construction, whose horizon is illimitable.

> There is a grandeur in this view of life, [wrote
> Charles Darwin] with its several powers, having
> been originally breathed by the Creator into a few
> forms or into one; and that, whilst this planet has

40

gone cycling on according to the fixed law of
gravity, from so simple a beginning endless forms
most beautiful and most wonderful have been and
are being evolved.

There is one primary test for any religious philosophy, and
one which few have withstood. It is that of explaining suffering, pain, unhappiness, *la misère de la vie*. The virtuous man
is happy, said the Stoic, who identified virtue with knowledge. And much religious doctrine — Judaic, Christian or
Muslim — is not very different. Virtue is its own reward. 'I
have been young, and now I am old, yet saw I never the
righteous forsaken, nor his seed begging their bread.' It is, as
Fielding remarks, 'a very wholesome and comfortable doctrine, and one to which we have but one objection, namely
that it is not true.'

Clearly there is more to it than that. To postulate a Power
behind the world which is both omnipotent and good is to
impale faith upon the horns of a dilemma. And however
ingenious the doctrinal apologetics of the monistic religions
which make these hypotheses — and some have been extremely ingenious — none of them succeeds in satisfying the misgivings of minds not already committed by religious faith.

Our universe of progressive structural development, of
self-creative ideology, cannot stand if this problem cannot
be faced. If a philosophy of life cannot supply the art and
rationale of living, then all else matters little.

It is noteworthy how even the most convinced pessimist
recognizes everywhere the demand for happiness. Happiness
is the norm, as Good is the norm, however inadequately
individual experience realizes the norm. It is the pessimist's
complaint, not that the world is very evil, but that it falls
short of reasonable desire and expectation. Unhappiness,
undeserved suffering, excruciating physical or emotional
pain, however commonly and bitterly they may be experienced, are the exception, not the rule of experience. People
generally, rightly or wrongly, expect to be more happy than
unhappy. If we are to see things as they are, we have to
recognize that Happiness is identified with Good, and
Unhappiness with Evil; the latter is regarded as a matter or
occasion for complaint, protest or amendment much more
than the former is regarded as a momentary respite snatched

from a maleficent Providence.

Probably the most complete happiness to a human being is a sense of adequacy, when nothing falls short within himself, when everything is in line and in order, and he appears, almost effortlessly and inevitably, to hit the mark. In this sense of adequacy, this 'unity of being', we come near to our structural principle again, and here the whole lies in the equipoise of the personality, the unity of the man within himself as he faces his environment, with just that bias and orientation which we have hypothesized as in the nature of things. He is, for the moment, at one with the course of the universe, riding the crest of the wave with no cross-current, conscious or unconscious, to impede or thwart him.

It is a precarious thing, and by no means easily or frequently achieved. It comes to some, and at some times, as 'a sense of something far more deeply interfused'; the feeling that 'it is good for me to be here', arises from some deep inward awareness of response, and not from conscious thought. We owe to it some of the best in our literature; the sense of communion with nature that affected Wordsworth, or of identity with the divine that inspired the metaphysical poets of the seventeenth century. To others, artists and craftsmen of every sort, it comes with creation. To saint and mystic it seems to come as an exaltation and a secure content, and probably to these alone is it more than a passing wonder.

But these heights are not common; they represent the successes, the high spots in human experience which raise the ordinary level of more or less unconscious adjustment to, congruence with, their surroundings which makes most people's lives most of the time passively rather than actively happy. And, as one would expect, though they are qualitatively less important, the failures — or rather the lack of positive successes — in the relation-making process which makes up the individual life, are quantitatively more numerous, and with them comes consciousness of incompleteness, of disharmony, of discontent, or, most common of all, accidie, that most mortal of all sins. It is, after all, entirely in accordance with the process that we have been discussing that there should be more misses than hits; what is perhaps surprising and encouraging about the mental life — what makes happiness rather than unhappiness the norm — is that there are as many hits or near-hits as there are.

One last point in this long digression. If all this is not merely an attractive speculation for the philosophic dallier and dilettante, we must guard ourselves against two impulses. The first is to plunge into abstractions, treating concepts as independent entities, with no connection either with the physical world or with each other. We have already, for convenience of analytical discussion, strayed dangerously near the edge of this precipice, and some may feel that we have gone over the edge. The second is to use the word 'reality' lightly. What do we mean when we say that values, spiritual verities, may attain a reality of their own?

There are two answers. First, to quote Butler, 'everything is what it is and no other thing'. We can no more deny the reality of the psychical experience of mankind than we can deny the reality of the physical. If the one is real, the other is real; if the one is illusion, the other is illusion — and the illusion has still to be accounted for. We may quarrel over the labels that are by their nature nothing more than symbols, reflections of our own inherent limitations in attempting to express in speech or writing degrees of subjective consciousness that transcend these rational media. It is like trying to navigate by Euclidean geometry; one is in the wrong — or at least inadequate — frame of reference; we have got into a world in which we do not, and perhaps cannot, know the techniques of measurement and communication as we are accustomed to interpret them.

Mind, psychologists tell us, is composed of conscious and subconscious, the latter being a vast field whose influence on the personality is all the more powerful because we cannot see it at work. It does not seem to be doing violence to our reason to conceive that certain factors in our psychological make-up, certain feelings whereof we are conscious but which we cannot fully explain, have their roots in this field. What we call association, instinct, intuition, and that subtle sense of unity with the substance of things unseen, may — we cannot go further than this — fall into this category. All of these are capable of a reasonable explanation; they may represent centuries of memory, thought and habit crystallized into subconscious knowledge. It is possible, even probable. But what we have to accept is that, whatever their origin,

43

such perceptions render instantly available to us knowledge, capacity for decision or feeling, to arrive at which conscious reasoning would take far longer and more cumbrous methods, if, indeed, it could arrive at all. An analogy might be found in the human embryo, which passes in a few months through many stages of evolution. Nature — the creative process of development which has been our main theme — does not continue to go over all the old ground in the same laborious manner; there is, as it were, a brief recapitulation, a rapid summary, and then the new start is made some little way further on.

To pass on. We have postulated the evolution, from what we call matter, of life, of mind, of personality, of values. All we must regard as real, if we regard ourselves as real. All are in accordance with that bias, that structure-making orientation that we have stressed all along as inherent in the nature of things. To assume a still more complex creation in the making, characterized by a greater capacity for experience, a greater diversity of powers, and a greater independence of environment, is to fit in with both fact and theory. We may call this creation soul or spirit, but we must be careful in doing so to avoid theological connotations.

This spirit of man has an independence greater than that of the mind, although in personality both are intimately bound up. Has it an absolute independence of the physical body? We saw the mind as partially independent; is the spirit, with its even wider field, altogether so? This is the dark question of immortality, to which none except the devout believer may venture to give a certain answer. But to me — and this is given very tentatively — looking back on the chain of thought which has gone to make up this conception of the nature of things, it does not seem impossible that those in whom the things of the spirit have been most strongly marked should attain a life and a reality not co-terminous with their mere physical identity. For the great majority of the human race, spiritual consciousness is not nearly vivid enough to hope for any form of survival after the dissolution of the physical frame that houses our largely inarticulate and inconsistent strivings. But that those in whom the pulse of the universe beats most strongly; who have in their physical lifetime a strong and persistent sense of unity with a process greater than themselves; who order their being after that way — that these should in some sense survive would not be strange. For they would be indeed the fittest.

7   The Concept of a Rational Good

We are now coming near the end of the first part of our long and vagrant quest. I have said that any metaphysic must be to a large extent personal. For the outlook on life and the nature of the universe contained in the preceding two chapters, no validity is claimed except that to me personally it does provide a coherent explanation of things that are necessary to our peace.

It remains to link up this personal metaphysic with the empirical moral code which, it was suggested in Chapter 4, dominates, more or less unconsciously, most people's behaviour. This code constituted a sort of common ground of ethics not static, nor inclusive, but a fairly persistently accepted measure of social approbation. The qualities thus approved were: Reason, Understanding, Judgment, Integrity, Courage, Charity, Strength, Humility, Order.

Now the qualities that seem to emerge as having evolutionary significance — i.e. as having a survival value which gives as much of an objective index to ultimate verities as we are likely to get — are the qualities which realize, through successive experiments in relationship-making, new integralities with new capacities and potentialities. In human terms, this process comes to have a moral content. If there is in fact an orientation and a direction to which a capacity for self-development and creativity is integral, then obligation enters in as soon as this is consciously perceived. If that were not so, then Mind might become self-destructive. Mind is that stage in the process at which the process ceases to be wholly blind; self-direction becomes possible, and the process is thereby accelerated or retarded. If moral obligation means anything, it implies that a furthering of the process is good, and a hindering, or even a passivity, a non-exercise of the moral sense, is bad. This appears, on the premises given, to be the only metaphysical foundation for Ethics, and to me it is inescapable.

Now what, in applied morals, does this mean? It would seem to mean, first and foremost, a respect for life in the widest possible interpretation of those words. The process through which the depths and breadths of human experience have become possible is not one to which the human mind can at any stage set limits; experiment is the substance of creation; it is the means of grace and the hope of glory. We cannot arrogate to our own range potential capacities for expression, possibilities of new ranges. This is surely basic; the denial of this infinite potentiality of life seems to me to be the ultimate evil, the unforgiveable because irreparable sin designated in Christian theology as the sin against the Holy Ghost, its affirmation expressed equally in the phrase 'have life, and have it more abundantly'. Loss and destruction of life is in nature inescapable; it is part of the process of trial and error, hits and misses. But deliberate or capricious destruction of life, whether it be from the vanity of the murderer, the self-righteousness of the sovereign state or the exhibitionism of the sportsman, is morally detestable. It is *avoidable* destructiveness, with no compensating or potential gain; it is not only actual life that is destroyed, but the capacity for life; the quality of future experience which might have enriched its possessor, and, through him, the world, is not assessable. This is not to say that all killing is morally unjustifiable; this would be to ignore a whole range of conflicting moral obligations in which the sacrifice of the individual life, human or animal, may be the least of available evils. But it is not something we should ever be happy about. The Puritans, Macaulay tells us, disliked bear-baiting not for the pain that it gave to the bear, but for the pleasure it gave to the spectators. The Puritans were, if for the wrong reasons, perfectly right. For a morally conscious being to find satisfaction in destructiveness is for him to take the attitude of active negation; he is setting himself against the stream of creation, and doing violence to his own capacity for future creativeness.

Second, if the structural tendency, the bias that we have posited, is fundamental, individuality must be regarded as a Good: a sense of one's own powers, with a sincerity and

47

force to express and realize them, since only by such expression and realization can the bounds of individuality be widened. And this implies a very alert regard for individual integrity and even for individual eccentricity in whatever minds these be found.

Third, chaos and anarchy must be regarded as retrogressive, and Reason, Judgment and Order as Goods. This implies more than the need for orderly environment, a condition of good governance in which individuality may develop; the existence of laws creative of liberty which are also, in Bentham's phrase, necessarily abrogative of liberty. It implies, even more fundamentally, the rational method in human intercourse, the negation of caprice, the clear appraisal of desired ends and self-consistent means.

Now the parallel which we have here is surely rather remarkable. The empirical ethic of history and everyday life, and the ethic reached on metaphysical premises, are found to be in essence almost identical. Once more, we should be on our guard; we cannot really get outside the phenomena we are studying, and the parallel, in any proper scientific sense, is not worth very much. Our minds will, in the last resort, prove what they want to prove. Nevertheless, processes of coherent thought can do something to check this; there is, in Lowes Dickinson's phrase, the disinfectant discipline of rationality which is not entirely worthless in that it at least demands certain elementary canons of self-consistency which must satisfy other minds than our own.

Thus it now remains for us to examine this apparent correspondence and, finally, to draw what conclusions seem legitimate and necessary in the application of the ethic to education.

Now what I have called respect for life implies, first, sensitivity. It is, fundamentally, the capacity for response, the quintessence of the potentiality for making relationships. It is the power to identify oneself, at least momentarily, with another personality, to get inside someone else's skin. Its negation is self-centredness, callousness, hardboiledness. It is also the intuitive quality of being aware without being told, and as such it is a qualitative extension and intensification of experience. What we earlier defined as Charity is inherent in it; Tolerance is part of it, though perhaps a rather passive and pallid part. Humility is implied in it, the recognition of a limitation of faculty, and a reaching after increase; the opposites again are arrogance and self-sufficiency.

I have said that self-centredness is the negation of sensitivity, and yet also that individuality is a Good. Both these things are true. Self-centredness is more often the consciousness of a small ego than of a large one; its victim is too little, not too much, an individual. Individuality is in fact the balance; it is the equipoise, probably and usually temporary, in which a just realization of oneself and one's own powers makes possible an extension of that self and a development of those powers. It is in fact the framework in which sensitivity can have play. That is its importance, and that is why individual integrity is a prime Good. Strength, therefore, and Courage, and even a certain ruthlessness are Goods, if the individual be clear about the end, which is himself-in-relation. In the last resort, self-sacrifice may be more of a vice than self-assertion; I must be what I am and can reach out to be, if I am to be anything at all. The danger that this may be abused, and self-realization be perverted to arrogance or callousness, is not an argument against the equipoise of a positive individuality as the ideal. Saints and geniuses have never been comfortable people to live with; one must take the risk.

Third, as I have suggested, the structure-making tendency implies order. The behaviour of phenomena is determinate; scientific generalizations acquire the character of law. Respect for, correspondence with, law comes to have, therefore, a survival value; the truth of this in the limited field of human society is well demonstrable, where political units become capable of disregarding the laws of their own coherence, and thus of self-destruction. Here again the question of balance is cardinal. The claims of individuality may conflict with the claims of order; the claims of larger loyalties may conflict with the claims of lesser. This is the region of political science — in educational terms again of real importance — and it may well be that such conflict is genuinely tragic and irresolvable, conflict between two rights. There may arise, for an individual in a state or in a school, a fundamental duty of disobedience, if he is to be true to his conception of his own powers and obligations, and for society a fundamental duty of repression, if his action or attitude looks like disrupting the terms in which social coherence can alone be maintained. This question is an important one, and will have to be taken further in the next part of our study.

But the idea of law and order goes much deeper. The faculty whereby law may be perceived and developed, and the faculty whereby men may consciously further the process of which they are a part, is that which we call Reason. The evolution of consciousness imposes the use and cultivation of the rational faculty as a moral obligation. Not only is it for us the chief, and in many respects the only instrument by which the business of human intercourse can be carried on, but it is the indispensable instrument for the further development of human knowledge and experience. It seems to me necessary to stress this, first because people in general so take Reason for granted that they are unwilling to rank it high as a virtue, and second because in our day, in both politics and the arts, there is a tendency to stress self-assertion and anarchic violence at the expense of Reason, with disastrous results.

Now if all this is justified, it seems that we can attach to the words 'Good' and 'Bad' very much more definite meanings than we in our generation are accustomed to do. Certain qualities and actions become 'Right' or 'Wrong' independent altogether of the particular preferences of individuals or the particular fashions and expediencies of society. There exist standards by which legitimate judgments may be made; actions may be performed wilfully, and opinions given capriciously, but the standards remain unaffected. There are, that is to say, intellectual grounds for holding that values exist, however inadequately they may be recognized and interpreted.

This is an important theoretical step. How important is it in practice? After all, we have been emphasizing all along that life as lived is social life, and what people mainly need and desire is a practical interpretation of their contemporary social ethic, rule of thumb guides of a more straightforward kind than the highly abstract qualities which we have been discussing.

And for this, we have to admit, we are little or no further on than we were before. Even if we have established to our intellectual satisfaction that Virtue may be defined as the sensitive and constructive expression of individual integrity and equipoise, we are very far from being able to say what these words mean in terms of day to day behaviour. And we have to go further, and admit that on such a basis as we have laid down we are never likely to attain any cut-and-dried ethical code. One may well forgive a practising educator feeling more than a little impatient at having been led so far, and along roads so apparently roundabout, only to arrive at that same door wherein he went.

For the standard we have set up is, to the educator's mind, a peculiarly unsatisfactory one. It is, at one and the same time, both absolute and relative; there is no getting hold of it; no objective list of virtuous and vicious actions can be drawn up from it; no Tables of the Law come down from these rarified mountain heights. When we try to pin it down, it wriggles, protean, from our grasp, and changes its form. We tell the educator that a standard exists, independent of personal preference or of social expediency; we tell him in the next breath that there is no means of his defining, on any given occasion, what that standard is, because it is ultimately one for the individual judgment, of balance within the individual himself. Fundamental qualities remain as criteria of judgment in the background; in action we can claim only that the individual be satisfied *in his own mind* that he is interpreting them to the best of his ability.

Now we must grant all this, and at the same time point out first, that it is possible to overstress the difficulty, and, second, that the unsatisfactory nature of an ethic that is based on attitudes rather than on actions is an argument that would apply to almost every ethic worth considering. 'Ama Deum: fac quod vis', said St Augustine, and both Christian and Islamic doctrine is full of implications of a service, founded on internal surrender, that is also perfect freedom. Kant's 'moral law within', and the Socratic 'know thyself', are equally subjective. Unless one is to be content with a Procrustean formalism, a Pharisaical emphasis on the letter of the law or an arid collection of post-Confucian adages, one has to agree that in the last resort morality is, from whatever angle, a personal thing. One may achieve the mass-production of conventional observances, but the substance of morals remains intangible and internal:

51

> there is no royal road
> to save souls by the barrel load.

The limitation is one that causes parents and teachers especial perturbation; there is an almost irresistible temptation to identify morality in children with the performance of approved actions, whereas the two are commonly, though not always, unrelated, and the attempt to achieve the one through the other is likely to be not only futile but even positively harmful.

Yet the indeterminacy of this relative-absolute code that we have outlined does not make it practically worthless. To have to justify your actions to yourself and to others in terms of coherent law, and not to be able to plead either caprice or convention as sufficient answer, is in practice a stringent requirement. The occasions of *genuine* conflict, given the assumption of rationality, should be rare. Most people do in fact wish for the approbation of others, and one's own conscience has to be singularly clear and decided to justify cutting across or defying a considered social judgment. The point is that it must be considered; that is a fundamental obligation for all parties. And this obligation to stop and think over both the performance and the judgment of an action is the bridge between theory and practice; it is the anti-toxin against the twin poisons of interested self-deception and jealous conventionality to which, in moral issues, individuals and societies are prone. It is by implication a recognition of common standards, an admission of their existence and their validity. The only dubieties and obscurities that then remain are those of interpretation and synthesis, and interpretation and synthesis are both rational processes.

Means   Part two

The wits that dived most deep and soared most high,
  Seeking Man's powers, have found his weakness such —
Skill comes so slow, and life so fast doth fly;
  We learn so little, and forget so much.

Sir John Davies

I am a part of all that I have met;
Yet all experience is an arch, wherethrough
Gleams that untravell'd world, whose margin fades
For ever and for ever when I move.

Alfred, Lord Tennyson

Education is Discipline for the Adventure of Life.

Alfred North Whitehead

We have learned the answers, all the answers;
it is the question that we do not know.

Archibald MacLeish

The preceding part of this study has not been directly concerned with education. Starting with the unsatisfactoriness of the existing position to traditional and 'progressive' educators alike caused by the lack of a positive or coherent ethic in education, it sought to suggest a way in which, for the rational humanist, it might be possible to construct one that was at once scientifically tenable, metaphysically consistent, and empirically satisfactory. In this second part, which sets out to deal with some of the more important practical aspects of education, I shall be assuming, not necessarily the validity in any ultimate sense of such a Rational Good as I have sketched, but merely its greater convenience and utility as a provisional hypothesis compared with either the negative ethic of 'good is a matter of personal preference', or any absolute code based on religious tradition which involves a much greater initial act of faith.

I make this assumption for the reason that whereas the philosophy or practice of education is hardly susceptible of profitable examination if either an anarchic or an authoritarian position is maintained — since there are no grounds for pursuing any issue beyond the first fence — the idea of a rational good provides a touchstone for both theory and practice that may be found useful.

It will be found, I think, that two interesting things at least emerge; a much greater similarity in underlying assumptions between the traditional and the modern than one would gather from the tenets of either, and also a much greater inconsistency within the assumptions and tenets of each than one would expect from the common generalizations made. I shall in this discussion be chiefly concerned with the so-called 'progressive' school, because the ideas underlying this are already of great direct and indirect importance which seems likely to increase; even in my lifetime conventional and traditional education has become increasingly influenced by progressive ideas and methods. Equally I shall be concerned with it because it seems to be the progressive type of school which suffers most conspicuously from negative or confused ethical principles. An uncritical attitude in a traditionalist institution causes neither surprise nor much concern; an uncritical attitude in a professedly progressive one, before which the traditionalist is on the defensive, is a serious matter.

The first and most fundamental assumption in every type of educational system is concerned with the nature of the human being. A basic assumption which our society inherits from religious tradition is that of Original Sin, and this has always been reflected in our schools. There is assumed, that is to say, a natural tendency towards wrongdoing which can be eradicated only by the acquisition of Grace. And in the traditional religious view one of the chief instruments of Grace was the persistent mortification of body and spirit which it was the duty of teachers and parents to impose upon the child. This assumption is seldom now explicitly affirmed; mostly it is denied, but it is still in fact reflected in much conventional school practice. It is impossible to consider the ordinary framework of school rules, punishments and rewards without concluding that 'bad' is regarded as more natural than 'good'; impossible to see the way in which children's time is mapped out for them in work and play save as the uncritical echo of 'Satan finds some mischief still for idle hands to do'. Left to themselves, it is commonly agreed in practice if not in theory, children will be lazy, dirty in body and in mind, selfish, mannerless, liars and delinquents. These tendencies represent original sin, and religion and education, precept and example, discipline and convention, games and prizes and competition have all to be utilized in the difficult technique of producing the moral and the social being. Note that I am not at the moment saying that this assumption is either right or wrong; I am merely saying that it still exists, largely unconscious and unexamined and mostly in an attenuated form, but in greater or lesser degree of practical application throughout a large part of conventional home and scholastic life.

Reaction from this conventional outlook has a history much older than that of the progressive school. There were sixteenth-century schoolmasters like Ascham and Mulcaster who, under the influence of the new humanism, questioned the value of traditional discipline, who pointed out that school ought to be truly σχολή, *ludus,* play, and not a place of restrictions and punishments and meaningless learning by rote. But the real theoretical attack on the underlying assumptions of religious tradition came with eighteenth-century Rationalism and eighteenth-century Romanticism, with agnosticism and *laissez-faire* and the Noble Savage and the Rights of Man. The human being is naturally good; it is his chains which corrupt him; sweep away the interests and abuses which inhibit and exploit the human spirit, grant mankind the 'natural rights' of liberty and equality, and the perfect society will emerge.

Bentham called this, which is all of basic importance in educational thought, 'nonsense upon stilts'. This gibe was not quite fair, seeing that Bentham's own sense upon stilts reached conclusions which, in their practical applications, were not very dissimilar, and that both Rousseau and Bentham owe an intellectual paternity to Locke. Rousseau and Bentham with their able disciples in educational theory, Pestalozzi, Montessori and, in our day most influential of all, John Dewey, are together responsible for modern education, a fact that explains much of both its strength and its weakness. Freedom is firmly held to be a Good, but the modern educationalist vaccilates between idealist and utilitarian grounds for holding it so, and ends up with one foot in each. Individual initiative and integrity must be respected in the child, but here again there is a doubt whether this rests on a romantic conception of the individual in himself, or whether respect for individuality is an educational technique, a means to an end. A policy of *laissez-faire* is regarded as likely to solve most problems, but the sense in which this phrase is used is left vague, and ranges from the reforming zeal of an early nineteenth-century Utilitarian to a mid-Victorian Panglossian complacency, a *solvitur ambulando* which has become the comfortable rationale for inactivity and irresponsibility. Children should be treated as equals; children are naturally good and naturally industrious when left to develop their own interests, children know what is best for them — and so on in this unexacting philosophy, until it becomes unclear whether the experience of the time-stained adult, who has moved so much further from the East, is to be regarded as a source of light or of darkness to the child — a question, for a school, of rather primary importance.

Now it seems to me that there is a case for more critical examination of both these fundamental attitudes, each of which I have for the sake of clarity deliberately simplified and sharpened, but not, I hope, to the point of distortion. Each seems to me to involve an unnaturally and unnecessarily large act of faith, and each becomes in practice so highly unrealistic that for each practice appears compromising and muddled. It is doubtful if any educator believes systematically in either attitude; what one finds is a certain predisposition which implies a preponderant background of one or other kind of assumption, while overlying this are numerous inconsistencies. A schoolmaster will sincerely believe in the essential 'worthwhileness' of his pupils, will feel it important to encourage responsibility and initiative, and at the same time will cling to a framework of discipline and an overt master-pupil relationship whose origin and justification lie in a wholly different view. Snubbing, making a child feel small, retributive punishment, insistence on deference, are in origin bound up with a particular philosophic and religious assumption about the human being; in education their place and function was clear as teaching the child his status in a cosmic hierarchy wherein he was at the bottom, with his schoolmaster, his father and God in positions of ascending magnitude. This cosmology is no longer held in set terms; it would, indeed, now be rejected and even ridiculed by nearly everyone, but the practices based on its premises persist in an emasculated form, and are justified on negative grounds that are really a rationalization of inertia, to the effect that an occasionally painful or humiliating discipline does a child no harm. Whether it does harm or not may be a matter for discussion; the point is that it was originally intended to do specific moral good for doctrinal reasons which few teachers or parents will now support but by which they are still unconsciously influenced.

And it is not only the great majority of conventional

teachers and parents who are so influenced; the enthusiasts for 'free' education are affected also. It is both a logical and a psychological weakness in the latter that they tend to under-rate the importance of the system that has produced, in them, its own reaction. While consciously reacting against their own educational background, they have precisely the same psycho-logical hinterland of emotional ties and traditional shibbo-leths as those whom they now oppose. The very violence of their reactions, their intolerance of orthodoxy, often gives them away. And the danger here is that the underlying atti-tude will get across to the children, while the surface sweet-ness and light, the rational liberalism which is the expressed reason for the school's existence, may be little but a senti-mental veneer.

But this may be by no means outwardly obvious; in educa-tion, as in medicine, the layman uses a pedestal as a means of shelving responsibility, and parents will not penetrate beneath the professional jargon which, especially if it is at all psycho-logical, they feel to be vaguely flattering. Teachers in general, and perhaps 'modern' teachers in particular, are prone to maladjustments; their profession, probably more than any other, cuts them off from people in normal non-academic jobs who tend to think that there may be more than a grain of truth in Bernard Shaw's dictum that 'those who can, do; those who can't, teach'. The non-teacher also, albeit semi-consciously and somewhat timidly, resents both the teacher's privileges — e.g., his apparently short hours and long holidays — and his greater vocabulary and intellectual facility. And the teacher is, in school, dealing almost wholly with minds inferior to, or at least less experienced than, his own.

Such a position is almost inevitably corrupting. The effect is that, fundamentally on the defensive, unsure what his abilities really are or even if his job is really worth doing, jealous of the far greater economic rewards of professions of similar standing, the teacher tends to build round himself a shell of intellectual arrogance, of which he may be — and often is — unaware, but which cuts him off still more effect-ively both from his fellows in the outside world and from his pupils. Since all this tends to cause him, or her, to be emo-tionally timid and sterile as well, the result is too often a thwarted and supersensitive individual who is more concerned with his or her own conflicts than with the actualities and needs of children's lives. Loss of efficiency apart, this type of maladjusted teacher — who in greater or lesser degree is far commoner than the layman suspects — is in two ways highly dangerous. The first way is that he is unconsciously in danger of practising what amounts to psychological rape on his pupils, reading his problems into their lives, demanding their affection, playing on their undeveloped emotions, setting up his approval as a motive and as a reward. And for 'he' and 'his' we must of course also read 'she' and 'her'. This type of teacher, in this degree of exaggeration, is more common in fiction than in reality, but it is none the less a fact that in mitigated and subtler forms he and she are very common indeed.

The second danger is less immediately obvious. Since the teacher's internal conflicts mean nothing to the children, the children must translate the attitudes they perceive in the adults surrounding them into the terms of their own experience. The result can often be a sort of generalized self-sufficiency, an aggressive and somewhat cynical individualism. Progressive school teachers often seem to imagine that if they deliberately refrain from imposing their ideas, they are leaving the children free to form their own. This, of course, is not so. Whether adults express their views or not, they are in fact influencing the children with whom they come in contact, since the children will in either instance learn the values which the adults around them think important, and will either adopt them, or, if they are presented too violently in either affirmation or negation, react against them. The strongest case for teachers having their own philosophy and being adjusted in their own lives is that only so can they be matter-of-fact and impersonal about important things, i.e., can influence without dominating. On this count the orthodox sometimes show up better than the modernists, since even an irrational anchorage is probably better than none.

Less fundamentally, also, the progressive teacher is liable to the pitfalls inherent in his reaction against his traditionalist background. He has explicitly renounced the theory that punishment and humiliation may have good effects on children, he believes — in my view quite correctly — that they can do positive and demonstrable harm. Nevertheless he has within himself the desire to humiliate, to get back on people and institutions which represent humiliations to himself in the past. Now the everyday business of instructing and controlling children involves considerable strain and expenditure of nervous energy — more for the modernist school teacher than for the conventional, because the former has deliberately deprived himself of a framework of automatic sanctions. When he and his pupils are fresh, good temper and reasonableness will usually gain the kind of order in which work is possible. But when he or they become tired and frayed, lessons become less interesting; he tends to lose his grip, and, with nothing to fall back on, it is a great temptation for him to become vindictive, moralistic or sarcastic.

Moral bullying, of a more or less subtle kind, is again not uncommon in schools which have turned their backs on corporal punishment or conventional impositions. It is probably worst in residential girls' schools, probably because such schools are more often than not conventional and accept without question traditional views of human nature; also, since many of the disciplinary techniques thought suitable for boys are conspicuously unsuitable for girls, a fetish of 'honour' takes their place, and by reason of some obscure secondary sex character girls are easy to bully in this way. But the same fetish in various forms, and under variously dishonest tricks of vocabulary, has penetrated the modern progressive school also. Its danger seems to me to have been inadequately realized; stupid and pernicious anachronisms though beating and lines and detention are, they may well, if administered unemotionally and automatically, be less harmful than the persistent penumbra of moral tyranny implied in clichés like 'better nature', 'playing the game', 'being co-operative' and the like. Nothing is more fundamentally immoral — or easier — than to appeal to a child's embryonic sense of morality in order to get him, and even more her, to do what you want; the child will respond but you are creating either a prig or a rebel.

It will have been manifest from all that has gone before that the educational ethic I am putting forward involves neither the assumption of original sin, nor the assumption of original virtue; it assumes only that the child is an individual human being in process of physical, mental and moral development. It suggests that it is the function and responsibility of the adult, teacher or parent, to help the child realize his fullest potential in all three fields. To justify making an appeal to a child's developing moral sense, it is essential that you should be reasonably sure that what you are demanding of him is really a moral request, and not merely a dodge on your part which he is bound sooner or later to see through and resent, and, no less important, that it is a request of a kind that the child himself has reached the stage of understanding and agreeing with. If that stage has not yet been reached, an order is far better — more likely to succeed and less likely to be resented — than a moral appeal. It is, for example, far better to say 'Shut up', than to say 'Don't you think you ought to be quiet?' He does not think he ought, but he is made to feel that he ought to think he ought, and his resentment at being made to feel morally uncomfortable will make him hostile to you and intolerant of authority, which the simple flat-footed imperative will not do.

But the progressive teacher is unsure of his ground here; he lacks confidence in his right and perhaps also in his wisdom in laying down flat-footed imperatives. He is not sure, to go back to our example, how noisy children should be allowed to be, because he has at the back of his mind a Rousseauist feeling about the instinctive goodness and wisdom of the untrammelled child, which has been reinforced in his training-college days by a great deal of uncritically assimilated jargon about freedom of expression and life-adjustment. Accordingly he rationalizes and reassures his own conflicting feeling about the educational desirability of a certain degree of quiet, by going back one stage to a social generalization which he considers should be obvious to the child also — e.g. 'People ought to be considerate of other people.' Either he is successful in the superficial sense of gaining his immediate objective, because he himself is sufficiently strongminded and because there is a school climate which favours moral generalizations, or he is ineffective, and finds himself involved in an argument in which his conclusions are a great deal clearer to himself and the child than the grounds for them, and the eventual result is an expense of spirit, a lowering of morale, and a residue of hostility and contempt.

This is not an argument in favour of conventional rules and punishments: very much the reverse. Nor is it an argument in favour of the use of the flat-footed imperative, which is a technique demanding extreme care and infrequent application if it is not either to corrupt the user or become ridiculous and ineffective. The point about it is that, used occasionally and with discrimination by people whose judgment the children respect as fair and sensible, who normally have good reasons for what they do and ask to be done, it is a better means of immediate compulsion than either a homily or a sanction because it leaves less resentment and tension behind. It is most successful where the issue is of immediate and practical, but not of vital, importance; theoretical issues which are, or may be, raised by the practical case can and should wait for proper discussion and elucidation. But the normal practical questions of school and home life involve secondary rather than primary principles; cleanliness, bedtimes, tidiness, punctuality, quiet, are matters of convenience and expediency; the ends which they serve are not seriously questioned by the normal child. To present these things in moral dress is asking for trouble; as part of an automatic framework of imposed routine they will be accepted or, to a not very important degree, evaded.

It seems to me important to stress that, except on a very small number of first-class questions involving clear and fundamental principle, the thing to be chiefly avoided in dealing with children — and most especially in dealing with adolescents — is any suggestion of moral content in word, tone or manner. And on those first-class questions — bullying, for example, is one such — the moral content should be explicit at the outset, and presented rationally and in such a form that the child or adolescent can discuss the issue without feeling that he is being got at, and without, as far as this is possible, loss of face. To say to a boy or girl. 'Aren't you being rather silly?' is morally offensive; 'Lay off, you' is morally neutral. That quality of moral neutrality, far more than educational technique or psychological insight, is probably the secret of the successful teacher; it is A. S. Neill's peculiarly valuable contribution to modern education.

The trouble about the flat-footed imperative is that, used more than occasionally, it becomes ineffective, and has to be reinforced by sanctions. And the trouble about sanctions is that, once he has them at his disposal, the teacher does not have to be rationally clear that he is justified in what he is doing or imposing. 'Power tends to corrupt; absolute power corrupts absolutely.' The most conspicuous and the most damning thing about punishments in conventional schools is that the worst teachers use them most. Whether or not the idea of punishment in education can be completely dispensed with I am doubtful; it is a question that I propose to discuss further later. But in pointing to the effects in adult society of the system of school punishments as they have been and are still, though to a much milder extent, known in our day — fear, resentment, intolerance, readiness to resort to force, refusal to accept arbitration, war-mindedness — the modern educator is wholly right.

Nevertheless, right as he is, the philosophy of the modern educator has remained largely a negative one; he has still to achieve a positive ethic which will give his convictions drive and direction. Conventional educational practice is vulnerable, because it is fairly clear-cut; it is part of a recognizable tradition carrying tenable, if frequently out-moded, assumptions and conclusions. Progressive educational practice is vulnerable for precisely the opposite reason; first, it depends too greatly on the personality of the individual educator who is often reacting against his own background; second, it derives from confused rationalist and romantic premisses which have no clear relation to each other, and which are not explicit to those who hold them.

Neither the assumptions of the orthodox school nor those of the modernist have yielded, in theory or in practice, a consistent or satisfactory answer to the primary question of the scope and function of school authority. But if we start with our own earlier assumptions, the position becomes at once both easier and more realistic. Reason is a good, and individuality is a good, but no major premiss is made about the essential nature of the human being except that he or she is a unit of experience with a capacity for constructive growth. And that growth, as and when it appears, is, *a priori*, also good. We lay down nothing about the child as such, except the rather important tautologous fact that he or she is a child who has yet to develop into a mature individual.

On this basis, the relation between child and adult begins to take on common-sense aspects. Neither child nor adult has 'natural' rights; each has the rights pertaining to his functions and potentialities as an individual and member of society. Of these the most fundamental is the right to grow — physically, mentally, morally. The child thus has the right — now publicly recognized and subscribed to by every civilized nation under the UNESCO Declaration — to education, education defined as the furtherance of growth, and this becomes a duty for society to provide. In so far as liberty is defined, as Graham Wallas defined it, as the opportunity for continuous initiative, then liberty becomes a right. But that definition implies a condition, a tacit contract; freedom is not a good or a right *per se*, and the child has no claim to a freedom which contributes neither to his own growth nor to other people's. This in its turn implies the duty of discrimination on the part of adult authority, and the progressive school does not always make this important distinction. A schould recognize freedom as a right, contingent, as all rights are, on its possessor doing in fact what he is in intention enabled to do; it should err, possibly, on the side of faith and magnanimity in continuing to use freedom as a technique even when it is abused, or when its results are slow and discouraging. For abandoning it implies a fundamental disbelief in the child, a conviction that in this or that particular instance one is dealing with a personality in which, for the moment at least, destructive or criminal or anti-social tendencies are dominant. If these tendencies persist, or if their manifestations become violent, it becomes doubtful if the ordinary school is the proper place for such a child; if they merely represent a phase, such as in greater or lesser degree nearly all children pass through around early adolsecence, then probably only certain aspects of liberty will, in the interests of the community, have to be curtailed. But this is all a matter of judgment. However much the sensitive teacher may and should lean over backwards in attempting to meet the needs of a developing personality, there can be no possible doubt of the right and duty of a school to give or withhold freedom in the interests of the children's own development, and both teacher and pupil are guilty of a sentimental irrationality if absolute freedom is made an abstract right. Given that the teacher is personally and technically qualified to be a teacher, it is part of his function to make his experience available to his pupils, and the Rousseau-Wordsworth romantic fiction of initial virtue and wisdom — and equally much of the modern educational jargon of the child-orientated school — are both philosophically and pedagogically nonsense. The moral question involved in the imposition of adult authority is not one of right, but of method: not one of ends, but of means. The argument against it is not that the child's *actual* judgment will naturally be better than the adult's — which is improbable — but that, first, the imposition of authority is inefficient as a means of promoting development, and, second, that the *potentiality* for development may be higher in the child than in the adult, and this potentiality may be aborted.

All this is to suggest that what education means is latitude for subjective experience within a framework of control, combined with the stimulus of objective influence without stultifying domination. This, like all definitions, is abstract and utopian; more concretely, I feel that the danger in progressive even more than in conventional schools is that the strong personalities among the teachers are too strong, and the diffident, too weak; since neither has a rationale of the use of authority, the former blithely and largely unconsciously overrides the doctrines that he professes, sometimes to the extent of arousing resentment both among his pupils and among his colleagues, while the latter, more scrupulous and less successful, excites anarchy and derision by his apologetic timidity.

I have over-painted both types, but the tendency is there, and it produces an emphasis on the personality of the teacher that obscures the real value of the system, makes for confusion and inconsistency, and is intellectually vicious in that subjects become identified with those who teach them. Of the two excesses, timidity is probably the worse; a domineering personality will probably produce a reaction, but there is nothing to compensate for the feeling of insecurity and cynicism which children get when they find those in supposed authority over them to be, in will or intellect, inferior to themselves.

Liberty, as we have inherited it — again with the double Romantic-Utilitarian background — is an unsatisfactory negative conception, if only because it sanctions an atomistic view of society that is unreal and undesirable. To the educator, freedom *for* what is a far more important question than freedom *from* what; that is why Graham Wallas' definition is so much better than John Stuart Mill's of 'doing what we like .... without impediment from our fellow creatures, so long as what we do does not harm them'. This is not to say that the child should be made continually conscious of the need to justify his actions or desires *sub specie aeternitatis* — that would lead to an intolerable priggishness. But 'It doesn't harm anybody else' is not *necessarily* a good or an adequate answer; it may be or it may not be, and the teacher's scrupulousness should lie not so much in abstention from interference — though this is normally desirable — as in an insistence that the occasion and grounds for rational choice should be there apparent for the child on any important issue, and it may even be the teacher's function and duty at moments to override the child's judgment. In these instances, the issue should be presented to the child not as a choice for him to

67

make, but as a decision already made, with explicit reasons. It is a dishonesty which children quickly see through if their decision appears to be invited on a matter upon which authority has already made up its mind. It is, in effect, the old 'Will you do this voluntarily, or shall I have to make you?'

What is the relation of liberty to equality? The two words have such close romantic associations that they tend, for good and ill, to get lumped together, and in education, as in politics, there is little attempt at rational discrimination. It is taken for granted that conventional education is authoritarian, and therefore anti-egalitarian in its outlook. Equally it is taken for granted that the progressive school is libertarian and egalitarian. Those who, from either side, continue to argue from these highly artificial premisses tacitly agree that the relation between the two concepts is simple and direct. But neither in theory nor in fact is it so. The English nation is an excellent example of a society with a high degree of personal liberty and a very low degree of social equality, while the Irish exemplify a fundamental egalitarianism with personal liberty narrowly restricted. Similarly, a Catholic religious community is highly authoritarian in both theory and fact, but given the framework the equalities within it are more fundamental than the inequalities. The Public School system in England is crammed with petty inequalities, and has the whole idea of social inequality, the production of an élite, a cadre of leadership, integral and basic to it. But given a level in the hierarchy, there is no difference in treatment between boy and boy, and place in the hierarchy is governed more by seniority or specific ability than by social class or parental wealth. Indeed, this lack of discrimination in the treatment of individuals is very largely what the progressive educationalist — as distinct from the now fashionable comprehensive school egalitarian — complains about; he claims it to be the first duty of a school to be aware of individual differences, and to be ready to apply, as it were, different sauces to different geese. And anyone who has worked in a progressive school will know the practical problems that in fact arise when a particular child's development demands preferential treatment of one kind or another, yet he must not be made to feel separated from his social or chronological contemporaries, nor must the group to which he belongs be made to feel that his privileged treatment is unfair to them. Here again there is inconsistency and confusion in the modernist outlook; in their justifiable anxiety to do away with irrational inequalities — prefectorial powers, fagging, privileges in dress or behaviour at certain levels; privileges gained solely by athletic prowess; exaggerated deference to elders as such; inequalities that are socially meaningless and pernicious — progressive school enthusiasts have tended to go, in this as in other ways, to the opposite extreme, and to claim for children equality with adults and equality with each other in all important respects. All deference to age or experience is discounted and discouraged, and social coherence and adaptability are prized at the frequent expense of the individual child's intellectual development. This is especially true of much American education, where school democracy tends to be carried to an extent that it is stood on its head, but the same thing is increasingly observable in English Primary and Secondary Modern education also.

Now in all this the progressive school is probably more right — except in its more flagrant excesses and inconsistencies — than it is wrong. If there is one piece of hypocrisy which it would be well to have categorically abolished, it is the lurking idea that there exists for children a standard or type of behaviour which adults do not consider necessary, right or reasonable to practise themselves. It is an idea that is remarkably persistent, and if one has to go to extremes to counteract it, then it is good to go to extremes. When an adult says that something is good for children, it is odds on that he is being consciously or unconsciously dishonest, and it is a kind of dishonesty that children notice and resent. Nevertheless, while it is important to stress that the same standards of right or wrong, good or bad, exist equally for children and adults, it is equally important to stress that children and adults are not equal, nor are children or adults equal with each other. Apart from the aberrations of doctrinaire professional educationalists, there is nothing in valid educational theory or practice to indicate that all children should be treated equally, anymore than there is anything in valid political theory or practice to say that all adults should be treated equally. On the contrary, there is a good deal to suggest that inequality of treatment, according to

69

definite and rational principles, is an integral part of education as of statecraft, and is essentially complementary to the democratic principle of equality of educational opportunity.

The rational principle is that where inequalities of treatment are applied in education, they must be inequalities based on the very things that distinguish the child from the adult, or the child from the child. Privileges which adults — or older or more advanced children — have, and young children do not, must bear some specific and direct relation to the work or responsibilities which adults and older children have to undertake and young children do not. Inequalities, that is to say, must, like liberties, be functional; those inherent in an older-younger relationship by reason of the difference in age or experience. There is no injustice in the adult deciding his own bedtime, and the child not being allowed to do so, because the balance between sleep and work or play is one which the adult, because he is an adult, is competent to decide, and the child, because he is a child, is not; it is something which he has to learn. There is injustice, on the other hand, in an adult breaking into a child's occupation and sending him off to post a letter, because in this instance the adult is using his age in a purely irresponsible and irrelevant manner. These are extreme examples, and consequently easy; in everyday practice it is frequently very difficult to decide the lines of demarcation between legitimate and illegitimate inequalities of treatment. But at least we can be clear on principle and motivation. The qualities desirable in children are the qualities desirable in adults; there is fundamentally only one set of values.

This is a lesson which parents and teachers learn with great reluctance, and this is why the progressive school is more right than it is wrong. Age brings no licence; rather the reverse. It is right and legitimate, up to a point, for children to exploit adults — and equally, beyond that point, for adults to resist exploitation; getting a just sense of one's own powers is one of the chief things in the difficult discipline of growing up. But it can never be legitimate for adults to exploit children; they should have achieved that sense and that discipline, and if they have not done so they are better away from children. The adult who gets a satisfaction of power out of his relations with children is inevitably cramping and warping the growing powers of the children themselves. The nagging, the sarcastic, the hearty and the psychological all commit this crime; the fact that most of them justify and rationalize their actions and attitudes under the cloak of adult responsibility only adds dishonesty to their other vices. It is a type of dishonesty with which, where it goes deep, it is almost impossible to deal; one can only be thankful that children are on the whole so tough.

But, when all this is stressed, one has to go on to acknowledge that real inequalities exist, and that recognition of them is educationally important. Treating children as equals is just as dishonest, if not nearly as harmful, as exploiting them or treating them as morally and intellectually inferior beings. Adults in charge of children have responsibilities that are genuine and inescapable, and when all the adult's liability to the abuse of power is admitted and discounted, the need for a positive attitude remains.

The metaphysic which we have put forward suggests what that attitude should be. The end for which the teacher and parent is — or should be — working is the integrated personality of the child, the optimum balance of powers of which his charge is capable. This, which is the goal for himself, is the goal for the child also; the same set of values is valid for both and for the same reasons. But the inherent inequality in their relationship lies in the fact that they are necessarily at different stages — stages of achievement, and, what is even more significant, stages of capacity for achievement. Although adults and children differ between themselves probably more than the morally sensitive and intelligent child differs from the morally sensitive and intelligent adult, nevertheless this point of capacity for growth is very much more important for children than for adults; it represents a genuine functional difference. The child's chief function is, after all, growing up; the adult's is using the growth he has achieved to the best advantage, and increasing it as and where he may.

There is, therefore, a qualitative as well as a quantitative difference that age and experience make between the adult and the child. This renders the means that the adult employs to help the child's development of very great importance; at different levels of age and experience and growing awareness of his powers that the child reaches in the formative years, the adult has to use constantly developing techniques to keep pace with the child's own developing needs. Too few adults remember how strenuous a business growing up is. The process of relation-making and breaking, of change and adjustment, of a succession of acutely felt failures and successes, is one which the adult likes to think, as early as possible, that he has put behind him; childhood, far from being the happiest days of one's life, is a welter of fears, uncertainties and instabilities, sudden self-confidences and devastating timidities. All this is because potentialities are still unfixed, and both constructive and destructive impulses are more violent than they normally are in adult life. Furthermore, and because of this, the right balance for the individual is somewhat different. Sensitivity is a latish development in personality; it can flourish only when a minimum of individuality is felt to be secure. Parent and teacher have therefore to realize that children are right in their tendency to be more self-assertive than adults; they have to be on their guard about the way in which, and the degree to which, they attempt to suppress this assertiveness. They should not expect, especially at the stages of maximum instability — around five and in early puberty, for example — such virtues as humility or tolerance or considerateness in any high degree from children's undeveloped personalities, however necessary and proper it may be to expect these virtues and to help children to acquire them at a later stage. The function of the adult in education seems to me to be precisely this: to be himself sensitive to the individual phases of development among the children with whom he has to deal, and to expect from them what, and only what, is intellectually and morally, as well as physically, justifiable and suitable to that phase.

From a very early stage the 'stop and think' requirement is suitable, and should be exacted. At the same time the adult should realize that there are only a very few things that a small child really wants to do that he or she should not have the opportunity of doing. Even this phrase 'really wants to do' may conceal an unjustifiable imposition of adult will, if the adult uses it in such a way that he shows by his manner that he 'really' disapproves. This is a counsel of perfection for nearly all of us; nevertheless, it is something to be borne in mind. The experiments a child must make in developing his personality inevitably involve a great deal of inconvenience for those around him, and possibly some degree of danger for himself. This must be accepted, and adults should reserve intervention for the occasions when the inconvenience becomes intolerable, and the danger such that serious and irreparable harm may result.

In spite, however, of this warning, I think that the adult is justified in going rather further in helping the child's development than I may seem to have suggested above. He must be sensitive not only to the present phase through which the child is going, but his training and experience should also make him sensitive to the next phase, and it is his duty to suggest to the child's mind attitudes and actions — and the reasons for them — which the child is as yet only on the verge of grasping. This, as I conceive it, is what moral education must mean, if it is to mean anything at all. He is not entitled to push these new attitudes, to ram them down the child's throat, but he is entitled, and I would hold obligated, to explain to the child his reasons for thinking the values which he is now presenting to be superior to those hitherto accepted by the child. It is probably futile and possibly harmful, for example, to imply to a child of four or five a moral disapprobation of noise at meal times on the ground of social convenience and other people's sensibilities; it is not necessarily futile or harmful for a child of eight to be made conscious of these considerations. Fairness is a quality which is very quickly and early appreciated; justice comes long before generosity in the child's mind, and it is of the highest importance that adults should respect, and exact respect for, this cardinal quality in social relationships. The further stage of giving way gracefully, of not insisting on one's rights, of saving someone's face or of seeing someone else's need as greater than one's own — these are extremely desirable developments of sensitivity, but it is quite useless to suggest their desirability until the child feels thoroughly secure about himself and his relationships with his world, which may be never, and is certainly unlikely to be before the age of physical maturity. Obviously all purely chronological levels are misleading, and individual processes of development take place in different ways for different personalities. A child may, for example, for quite personal reasons — possibly of parental background or example — be relatively mature and perceptive on some issues, self-assertive and defensive on others. As indeed happens in adult life; there is no demarcating line, and there are sides to all of us that never grow up. But it remains true that development along all lines is likely to be especially rapid in the formative years of childhood, and it is the fault of the adults concerned if potential development does not take place.

The moral obligation of the educator, we have insisted, is a positive one; he must be scrupulous and wary about it, but *laissez-faire* is not enough. Yet, in practice, all that the educator can do at any given moment is to exact or prohibit, encourage or discourage, the performance by the child of a particular course of action. How much good is this going to do, either to the child himself, or to the society of which he is a member?

Now on the relation between the performance of socially accepted actions and the growth of a moral disposition, both conventional and progressive schools seem somewhat uncritical. The former appears to retain the Arnold view — though with next to nothing of Arnold's conviction — that the atmosphere of a traditional moral code, backed by orthodox religion and maintained by the sanctions of divine and human punishment, tends to produce individuals more moral than they would otherwise be. There is, after more than a century in which the Arnold ideal has reigned supreme in the most influential section of English society, no evidence whatever to support this view, and the modernist school is wholly correct in pointing out that the ethical results in national and social life are negligible in comparison with the ethical paraphernalia employed in school; that, indeed, this moral code has tended to be counter-productive. A frequently hypocritical lip-service to dangerously outdated shibboleths is carried over into adult life, paralysing social reform at home and foreign policy abroad. And in the treatment by society of psychological delinquencies or perversions the traditional school attitude has done and continues to do incalculable harm.

In all important respects, therefore, the progressive school is right in suggesting that the exacting or prohibiting of specific actions will, at its most successful, lead only to those actions being done or not being done by a particular individual; it will not lead to the growth of a moral disposition in him, and, more important, it may lead to the development of other characteristics even less desirable than those which you are trying to remedy. But the progressive school proceeds to carry this unquestionably sound argument over to other and less fundamental issues where it is of more dubious validity, and there the conventional view, by the very reason of its conventionality, has something to be said for it. A conventionally imposed outlook on morality is bad, because it is all too likely to mean dishonesty and sterility at the core; it poisons the very springs whereby the individual can grow into a morally conscious being. A conventionally imposed outlook on manners is not necessarily bad, if the acceptance of a standard code of behaviour in matters that are not of themselves very important can lead to a greater harmony in social relations, and consequently make possible the growth of a sense of interdependence between society and himself which is an essential part of the individual's development.

It is perfectly true that the inculcation of conventional good manners may do no more than produce automatic reactions in the child, and that superficial courtesies may mask fundamental resentments, and leave a fundamental selfishness unaffected. We are all familiar with individuals, men, women and children, with charming manners who are as hard as nails underneath. But while this is an important truth, it is not the whole of the truth, and it is perhaps unfortunate that it has been uncritically accepted as a psychological commonplace, with no more to it, by the progressive school and the would-be enlightened home. The result has been an excessive timidity about the effect on a child's growing personality of any standard of behaviour at all. To say that it is both ineffectual and unjustifiable to force adult standards of behaviour on an unwilling and uncomprehending child is not the same thing as to say that it is immaterial how a child behaves. Yet much modern school practice, and especially much Kindergarten and Primary School practice in both England and the USA, appears to assume that the second statement is as incontrovertible as the first.

If adult non-interference and non-imposition of standards

meant that children were thereby enabled to grow up untrammelled, and to develop their own moral and social
standards without lurking resentments and selfishnesses,
there might be something to be said for this. But this is
romantic and illusory. The truth is that *some* conventional
standard exists for the child whether the adult wills it or no.
Conventional bad manners are as easy to acquire as conventional good manners, and experience seems to indicate a sort
of Gresham's Law about the currency of manners as of
money. Unless something is done about it, the bad will drive
out the good, and it has yet to be proved that the effect on
the child's moral growth is superior. Certainly we ought to be
scrupulous not to impose anything unduly foreign to the
child's capacity for comprehension. But equally the child is
acquiring experience and widening his comprehension all the
time, from our attitudes, positive or negative, expressed or
unexpressed, from his fellows, and from the prevailing convention in the school, which is the most impalpable but at
the same time the strongest influence of all. Tommy is not
necessarily going to grow up in moral freedom because we
refrain from expecting him to say 'thank you', or to close
doors behind him, or to wash his hands before meals, or to
wait for a pause in the conversation before he breaks in.
Tommy, finding himself in a situation in which it is apparently
'the done thing' not to say 'thank you', to leave doors
swinging open, to come to table with garden or workshop
grime on his hands and face, and to claim attention vocifer-
ously at all times, will be more likely to adopt these as his
values quite unconsciously and uncritically. And, later on in
life, he will have to unlearn these habits, which is a confusing
process, and one not without psychological dangers in its
turn.

Even if Tommy's own internal adjustments to life are
made smoothly and satisfactorily, and he acquires, as indeed
most children do acquire, a basic considerateness, the business
of having to revise and re-learn even minor social habits to
which the everyday world attaches social importance, is
likely to lead, for Tommy, to either resentment or snobbishness or both. He will justifiably charge the school with having
neglected one of its essential functions — i.e., with having

failed to make him aware of the nature of the adult world which he was about to enter. Equally he is liable to get the feeling that he has learnt to be progressive and intelligent about such matters, while the mass of society is conventional and stupid. In other words, he will be in danger of feeling permanently unsuccessful and isolated, and the conviction of superiority which he will cultivate to counteract this is not going to help his moral growth either.

These points are of real importance. Agreed, the imposition of a fundamental moral code is bad, first because this is something which the individual must work out for himself or it is valueless; second because, conventionalized, it is in certain respects manifestly insincere, and thus brings the whole concept of right and wrong into contempt; third, because the desire to please or the fear of punishment leads to conflicts and feelings of guilt which may have undesirable results in later life. But these are reasons against this particular kind of imposition; they are not reasons against any imposition at all. It is my contention that adult will or authority cannot, *per se*, be held to be unjustifiable; on the contrary, it may well be obligatory.

There seems to me to be a very great deal to be said for the exacting of usages clearly considered to be good, to the extent that this can be done without causing conflict in the child's mind, and even if taken separately the usages are of only minor importance. I advocate this partly because for most children the habitual performance of certain actions is likely to promote an attitude of mind unconsciously approving of such actions: what we do habitually we tend to take for granted as normal and right; and partly also because such usages can collectively establish an atmosphere of peace and repose, a framework of order in which more important mental and moral development becomes possible. In a world, too, in which violence is omnipresent, and gentleness conspicuously at a discount, it might seem worthwhile dropping some of our contemporary emphasis on the nobility of the natural and uninhibited individual, and returning in some small degree at least to the more civilized if more artificial well-bred rational humanism of Lord Chesterfield or of Confucius. Of the two tyrannies, good form is less intolerable than bad.

The Use and Abuse of Convention

But with all this the educator remains responsible for seeing that the individuality of any particular child is not going to be either stretched or lopped by a code designed for the well-being of the average and of the mass. Second, he remains responsible for ensuring that the code itself is constantly under constructive criticism, and capable of revision to meet new needs or new social emphases. The code of behaviour prevalent in a school is part of educational technique; it is a means to an end, not an end in itself. Consequently, the ends which the code is meant to serve must always be clear to the adult, even if they cannot always be so to the child, and the means must always be elastic.

Nor must the more easily enforced social virtues be allowed to loom too large, as they may well do because of their convenience to adults. Punctuality and tidiness, for example, are useful things; again, they can help to provide a framework in which more important ideas can be realized. But they are not all that important in themselves, and if they, or others like them, can be attained only by nagging, their utility is defeated. For the repose and kindliness which are the most necessary things in the child's background if he is to grow and achieve his own adjustments, are thereby destroyed. In effect, a convention of good manners is worth maintaining in a school, and it can normally be maintained to a very large extent without arousing conflict or resentment. But if the cost, in any particular instance, is conflict or resentment, then it is the convention and not the child that should be sacrificed.

11   The Ethical Basis of Coercion

We have got to the point of seeing the use of adult authority and the imposition of adult experience, or the abstention from their use and imposition, as matters of discretion and of technique, not matters of natural right. But since modern education has not squarely faced this, has never explicitly tackled the problem of the moral basis of authority, modern education is correspondingly never clear on the question that derives from it: what methods is a school entitled to use to ensure that liberties are respected and restrictions observed?

This secondary question is, after all, the important one in practice. If a conventional system of rewards and punishments is liable to lead to moral insensitivity and to unfortunate social consequences in adult life, a sentimental insistence on libertarian dogma leads to confusion, weakness and arbitrariness when, as is inevitable in any school, the practical point arises that certain restrictive regulations are essential. Even supposing that the restrictions in practice found necessary are so few and so rational that their necessity is self-evident to any child of normal intelligence who is brought to consider them; even supposing that they were, as is in many progressive schools the practice, decided upon by the children themselves in council, nevertheless, if the only sanction behind the rule is that the normal individual in his more thoughtful moments approves of it, then the result in practical politics will be that the rule will be broken on a considerable number of occasions by the dissident, the self-centred, the genuinely forgetful, and by almost everyone in his wilder moods. In so far as these infringements are relatively infrequent or unimportant, and the law can be substantially respected without sanctions coming into the picture, well and good. The use of compulsion, whether moral or physical, is always, in some degree, a confession of defeat for the principle of reason, and nearly always it leaves behind a residue of resentment against authority that is destructive to the development of that internal self-discipline which is or should be the school's moral objective.

But this is not to say that the whole question of the use of sanctions can be legitimately shelved, as modern education has on the whole tended to shelve it. Coercion or punishment is bad, not because either lacks moral justification — for that is demonstrably not true — but because by and large both do in practice more harm than good. Yet in the particular instance, and in the final resort, it must be clear that the right and indeed the obligation to coerce is vested in the school authority, and is inherent in the school's whole purpose and function.

Indeed, the question of authority and the use of coercion holds, for the school and the home, the same kind of moral problem as it does for the state. In both cases the individual is an involuntary member of an association whose ultimate ethical justification and aim is the rendering possible of the Good Life. It is not necessary to redefine here what is meant, in terms of our metaphysic, by the Good Life; that has been amply done already in earlier chapters. Any society which claims a moral basis for its existence must, in the person or persons of its executive, seek to provide for and reconcile the interests of the individuals who compose it. To harmonize and meet legitimate interests, and in the last resort to suppress criminal ones — i.e., those inherently destructive of the aims for which society exists or of its coherence, like murder, blackmail or wilful cruelty — requires the recognition of authority, and is the moral justification for the use of compulsion. It is even the justification in extreme cases for the elimination of the criminal individual from the society, when all techniques of reason or reconciliation have been exhausted.

A word of warning is necessary here. The function and scope of Authority is to *make possible* the Good Life, not to impose it. It has already been made clear more than once that Authority, whether in state, school or home, can do little *directly* to promote moral ends, and that if it attempts to do so it will, as many political and educational philosophers have pointed out, almost inevitably prejudice the moral predisposition by which alone the individual in society can achieve these ends. No amount of homilies on the virtue of truth-telling, for example, can alter the fact that

> A Truth that's told with bad Intent
> Beats all the Lies you can invent.

And so with all the virtues. All that Authority can and should do, once again, is to provide the setting, the framework, in which individuals can live and grow, and constructive relationships can be made.

First, in this connection, let us get rid of the rather persistent penumbra of loyalty as a morally desirable quality that hangs round the corporate identity of a school or of a state. Do not mistake me; I am not saying that loyalty to a cause or to an ideal is not a virtue; I am saying that loyalty to an institution can be — not necessarily is — a vice. Unless we are to give way to totalitarian ideology we must see every school and every state as having no value in itself; it exists to serve the specific purposes of specific individuals composing it, and it is deserving of loyalty to the extent that it does this, and no further. Allegiance must always be qualified by criticism, and it is important, in any social organization, that criticism should find voice; if it does not, the school will rapidly cease to serve any purpose save the self-importance of its directors.

For the harmonizing of the interests of a number of individuals, all in various stages of quickly changing development, is not easy, and while Authority is justified in abrogating liberties in order that the greatest common measure of liberty may exist, it is not justified in abrogating them because particular aspects of freedom are more important to the child than they are to the adult. The attitude of 'Go and see what Johnny is doing and tell him not to' is extraordinarily easy to fall into; very few busy adults do not have to resist an immediate impulse to say 'No' to a request that they vaguely feel may cause them further trouble. Further, the obligation rests with Authority not only to subject all demands made upon it to the test of reason, but also to take trouble and risks beyond the reasonable margin, because it is only through abnormal demands being made and met that common experience can be enriched and progress made. If the unusual and 'difficult' child cannot be fitted in, the school is to that extent failing in its function; coercion into a common mould, whether of academic attainment or of social behaviour, means not only damage to the child and a moral failure to the school; it is, far more seriously, a denial and betrayal of the values for which schools, like all human societies, should be standing.

Coercion, then, if it is to be applied, must be that degree and kind of coercion which is, first, intelligible to both adult and child, and, second, strictly necessary to attain the end in view. It is obviously necessary, for example, to have quiet, though not necessarily silence, in a library, and legitimate to enforce this, in the last resort, by withdrawal of the privilege of using the library. Equally it is unnecessary to have silence in the school corridors, and stupid to enforce this by fines or detention. In practice lack of funds, time and energy are the limiting factors which condition the means of any school to meet the manifold interests of children, however legitimate these interests may be; it is a very small minority of interests which are inherently impossible or wrong to meet, and which therefore have to be suppressed.

But there are some, and here again I feel that the progressive school may have leant over backwards too far in its understandable attempt to redress the balance from the practice and outlook of the conventional school. Malicious disorder and bullying are likely to occur at times in all schools as the expression of particular children's unsatisfied needs for reassurance or sense of power. The transgressor here plainly needs some degree of personal therapeutic treatment — not necessarily that of the professional psychologist — according to the depth of the trouble. Equally the rest of the community needs support and protection if the school is to fulfil its function towards them, and if the disease is not to become catching and finally endemic. The conventional reaction often tends to make the individual problem more acute by punishing manifestations of disorder instead of investigating the cause, but the progressive attitude may tend to sacrifice the interests of the community out of consideration for the special case. And the result may be — and too often is — to set up a recognized atmosphere of disorder and callousness which is both psychologically and pedagogically nullifying and destructive of the purposes for which the school exists.

Means

I am clear that Authority must be categorical about this, and must not permit such a condition to arise. If the individual impulse towards disorder or cruelty is strong, then the individual must immediately be removed from the group — not necessarily, of course, from the school, though that in the very last resort — and be treated in an appropriate fashion in a social environment to which in the meantime he cannot do such drastic or lasting damage. It may be stupid to punish cruelty, bullying, or malicious destruction, but it is equally if not more stupid to fail to step in and stop it at the outset with all the physical and moral force that may be necessary.

For this reason I am inclined to think that the progressive school's explicit condemnation and abandonment of the idea of punishment is both erroneous and somewhat dishonest. Here again the fact that progressive education is part of a reaction is important; those who practise it and believe in it are not seeing entirely straight. They are reacting, and quite justifiably reacting, against the more unintelligent and manifestly pernicious forms of punishment that they have seen or experienced in their own school lives. Hence their view of it as an educational technique is emotional rather than rational. They run the risk of taking up an absolutist position ('Punishment is always bad'), which is philosophically very difficult to sustain in any circumstances, and in practice impossible to sustain in conjunction with the claim that progressive education is both rationalist and experimental. The strongest reason for being clear-headed about matters of principle is the fact that any principle conditions all the rest, and that if one is not careful to see that the structure of one's convictions is a logical and self-consistent one, the hope of persuading other people, about things strongly held to be important, is remote.

With this confusion it is not surprising that in practice punishments tend to creep into progressive schools by the back door. They are seldom called punishments, and there usually remains a sincere if somewhat subtle and attenuated distinction in the minds of the school staff between punishments as used in conventional schools and the 'natural consequences' that replace them under a more enlightened dispensation. But in this the teachers are satisfying themselves rather than the children; being sent out of class for rowdiness, or having to make up for lateness at bedtime one night by being sent to bed earlier the next, while completely rational and intelligible to the child, are not in his eyes essentially different from punishments; they are merely the adult's idea of making the punishment fit the crime.

On the other hand, this ostrich-like unwillingness to admit the idea of punishment has its advantages, and it is possible that in practice these outweigh the theoretical confusion and intellectual dishonesty. A refusal to accept the fact that punishments are, or at least may be, valid methods of dealing with difficult situations where a child or a group of children is at odds with authority certainly tends to make teachers rely on reason as an initial approach and technique rather than merely on their own status and the authority that goes with it. They at least start off by being rightly critical of the conventional assumption that in any conflict between teacher and child the child is automatically in the wrong. Since, ethically, coercion should be the last resort, and since, practically, in progressive education it will be, the modern educator is probably on firmer ground than he knows. Power being the corrupting thing that it is, there is considerable danger that a teacher who is fully conscious of the rationale of punishment will resort to this much easier technique of asserting authority far sooner than is necessary or right.

Nevertheless, in the interests of intellectual integrity, the modernist should be made aware that there is no respectable ground for the view that punishment and coercion are always and of themselves unjustifiable; that this view if latent in a school administration may well result in feebleness of approach, inconsistency and insecurity, all of which are not only damaging to teacher-pupil relationships, but, even more serious, damaging to the conditions which are essential for the children's mental and moral growth. What really separates the modernist from the conventionalist is not, ultimately, a matter of fundamental principle, but a matter of timing and of technique; to the conventionalist the use of force is the obvious, automatic and immediate method of dealing with a knotty problem; to the modernist the use of force is a rare, *ad hoc* and the last resort: he will, if he possibly can, untie the knot rather than cut it.

Some schools attempt to hedge on the two values of freedom and order by making the children themselves the legislators, juries and judges of school laws. Two points of importance are involved here. First, there is an essential distinction between the children discussing, understanding, approving, and even initiating school legislation, and their being a sovereign body. This latter they cannot be, and again it is dishonest to pretend to them that they are. Morally and legally the school authorities are responsible for all that officially goes on in the school, and they cannot abrogate that responsibility. But it is manifestly desirable that children should be made politically and socially aware of the nature of and necessity for Law, and the presumption should be that only a highly exceptional school law — for example, one dealing with a physical danger whose gravity the children are, by their lack of experience, incapable of appreciating — should be put through without their understanding and assent. And by this I mean that the children, through discussion, should have an active comprehension of the issues involved, and not merely passively approve without accepting any responsibility. If punishments are normally ruled out as a technique of law-enforcement, then the treatment of misdemeanours, infringements of accepted law, becomes a corporate responsibility; not only the staff, but all the children themselves, are officers of the law, and this should be made clear as an essential condition to the absence of conventionally imposed discipline. And the implications of this should be explicit also, since they run counter to a very deep-rooted traditional feeling about school loyalties. As officers of the law, all members of the community, staff and pupils alike, are on an equal footing, and the traditional tendency of staff to support staff in any dispute, and for pupils to gang up with each other against staff, not only becomes completely illogical, but makes a system of collective responsibility and law-enforcement impossible to work. This may lead to situations of extreme difficulty and delicacy, in which a child's loyalties may be badly torn between the duty which he is conscious that he owes to the law of giving evidence about a misdemeanour that has been committed, and the impossibility he feels of 'splitting' on one of his fellows. This is why many schools, progressive as well as conventional, feel that it is better to have an impartial system of school justice wholly administered from above, rather than put children, whose mental and moral capacities are still being formed, into a position which may entail acute mental and moral conflict.

The second point about giving children responsibility for law-enforcement is this. There is another necessary distinction to be made between the school as a whole being consulted and the children expressing themselves on matters of law and its infringement — i.e., acting as effective public opinion — and their being given prefectorial or judicial powers. The latter is again unwise, for the reason not that they will administer the law too loosely or will be biassed, but that they are much more likely to be harsh, rigid, punitive, and undiscriminating between individuals. On the whole it is a mistake to give undeveloped personalities power over each other; it is likely to have a bad effect on the individual to whom power is given, and on those — often indistinguishable from him in understanding or experience — upon whom it is exercised. The detailed administration of the law in a school is best done, openly and explicitly, by the adults who have taken on the responsibility of being educators, acting as far as possible with the comprehending consent of the governed. And while laws should be few, and their administration tactful and discriminating, observance of the law can in general be fairly strictly exacted. Respect for law is not the highest of the virtues, but it is an important aspect of civilization, and a condition of a stable society in which growth is possible and other virtues acquired. In a school, the only way that respect for law can be inculcated is by the sure application of accepted rules.

12   Co-education

The progessive school is not always co-educational, but is very frequently so, just as it is the general, though not invariable, practice in conventional schools for boys and girls to be separated from the age of about eleven, if not before. This separation usually continues throughout school life, the two sexes meeting again for educational purposes, to a greater or less degree, at College or University. I am speaking, of course, only of the United Kingdom; on the Continent of Europe, and in the USA, there is no such differentiation as between conventional and progressive education; school life generally is co-educational, except in convent and seminary schools, military or semi-military academies, or schools deliberately imitative of the English Public School model. Equally I am speaking only of the present day. Apart from a very few early foundations, the Public School system in England and Scotland, and its concomitant, the Preparatory School, is a nineteenth-century innovation, as, indeed, is the whole state system of free and compulsory Primary — and to an increasing extent Secondary — Education. The Public School and the state-aided Grammar School reflected and continued the tradition in England that made education monastic for boys and domestic for girls; the tradition was, however, a matter of historical accident rather than of principle; any systematic education for girls hardly existed a century ago. Where educational provision did exist for girls as well as boys — as in the old Village or Dame School or Charity Schools — there was no idea of keeping the two sexes apart. Today, many if not most Primary, Secondary Modern and Comprehensive Schools in England are co-educational. There is thus no necessary connection between co-education and progressivism or radicalism, and it is a remarkable tribute to the influence that the Public School idea has had on the popular mind that today co-education is generally regarded as a strange, suspect and radical innovation.

Yet, curiously enough, the popular judgment on this is instinctively sound, though, as frequently, the reasons commonly advanced for it are thin and illogical. Co-education, as we find it in England and the USA in the twentieth century, *is* a radical innovation, because, linked up with Romantic-Utilitarian concepts of liberty and with the Dewey-ite concept of 'life-adjustment', still more, combined as it is in English progressive education with the nineteenth-century innovation of the boarding school, it now becomes a serious challenge to the traditional and, until recently, prevailing ethic of our late-maturing society.

The triumph of the Public School idea was not accidental; in its delaying of maturity, its sublimation, or, at least, attempted sublimation of adolescent sexual impulses into strenuous work and play in an atmosphere of sexual segregation, and its sanctions of conventional religion, it fitted admirably the culmination of that phase of expanding Western culture whose twin driving forces were Puritanism and capitalism. The now hotly-held and almost axiomatic assumption in England that throughout adolescence boys and girls should be separated as much as possible, and the animus behind the arguments commonly brought against the so-called 'free' schools, have their substance in a tacit but intuitively correct, if exaggerated, feeling that the ideas and practices of progressive education in general and of co-education in particular are undermining the whole complex fabric of the social and economic order. The almost equally strongly held view — in England, that is, not in the USA, where the reverse has been and is true — that even after school is left the responsibilities of marriage, home and children should not be allowed to distract a university student, male or female, during the years of concentrated and specialized intellectual development, has the same basis, and is only now slowly breaking down. Late sex development and late marriage have hitherto been regarded as integral to our culture.

The case for and against co-education, in effect, like the case for and against freedom in education, depends on assumptions which are on either side by no means always explicit and are frequently contradictory of each other.

Supporters of co-education usually base their arguments pragmatically on the fact that normal adult life is bi-sexual; men and women live and work together in society. It is therefore 'natural' to have boys and girls living and working together in school or college; to separate them is artificial, and surrounds each sex with an atmosphere of strangeness to the other which makes satisfactory relations in later adult life more difficult. Opponents of co-education base their arguments pragmatically on the fact that the sexual impulse in male and female develops long before it can be legitimately satisfied in the artificial but necessary conditions of civilized society, and that to bring boys and girls up together is inevitably to create emotional situations which will certainly be distracting and may be dangerous.

It appears to me that, as stated here, both cases are valid, and both are superficial and somewhat disingenuous. Artificiality in modern civilized society is not necessarily bad, nor is emotional distraction. All forms of common courtesy are highly artificial to the child until he has learnt to accept and practise them, while to large numbers of children pets, poetry or painting can be highly effective emotional distractions interfering with what a teacher or parent may consider to be the more important task of the moment. Both these arguments are in fact wholly question-begging, the appeal to Nature — with a capital N — ignoring the obvious fact, which the most ardent co-educationalist must accept, that most of what we regard as good in our civilization — transport and communications, medical care, mechanized agriculture, family planning, are only a few examples — involves the thwarting of Nature in a large number of ways; the appeal to Human nature — with a capital H — making the crucial assumption that the urge towards sexual intercourse is a dominant one from early adolescence, whereas it is the experience of educators in all types of school that, for the normal adolescent, other drives — physical prowess and intellectual curiosity for example — are far more dominant, and that the child, boy or girl, in whom the sexual urge is exceptionally strong will succeed in breaking through the framework of any institution, however rigidly segregated.

The co-educationist's argument about the danger of an atmosphere of strangeness, or of unsatisfied curiosity, has more substance, especially in a generation of small families. It is true that boys and girls brought up in a one-sex atmosphere tend to develop fantasies about the opposite sex — and about their own — which may make adolescence more unhappy, and later may make marriage less satisfactory, than need be. But it has to be pointed out that here the argument of each side is essentially, though from opposite angles, identical, for equally the apprehension of social and psychological danger in premature emotional relationships is a valid one. Both sides, that is, are concerned with the proper development and permanent happiness of the individual; they differ, openly, only about the means by which this should be sought and achieved.

But if excessive fantasy about the opposite sex is a psychological danger when the sexes are kept apart, so is no fantasy at all when they are thrown together. A complete factual familiarity with the physical, mental and moral attributes of members of the other sex is not necessarily an insurance against an unhappy marriage, as divorce statistics show. Equally the danger of premature emotional relationships is not necessarily averted by segregation. Homosexual relations, not necessarily physical but still distracting and upsetting enough, are not rare in either boys' or girls' schools, nor are they confined to emotional relationships of child with child. These points are important. Frigidity, auto-eroticism, cynicism, introversion, and a lasting sense of sexual insecurity or antagonism are more important things than either distraction or pre-occupation, and neither co-education nor segregated education can, of itself, guard against them.

In fact the whole discussion, on the lines that we have been conducting it so far — and these are the lines on which it is normally conducted — is artificial and unrealistic. I have deliberately omitted, incidentally, the argument commonly advanced at some stage by the opponents of co-education, that of the danger of schoolgirls having illegitimate babies, since it is statistically unimportant and ethically irrelevant. Pregnancies at school age occur from time to time, but rarely; they occur in co-educational schools, in the most strictly conventional girls' schools; they even occur in convents. However difficult a problem these isolated occasions may set for the individual family, the danger cannot be regarded as an argument either for or against co-education. The school-master who takes a party of schoolboys up Snowdon or Helvellyn is taking a physical risk greater than that of a school which mixes boys and girls together; fatal accidents happen on school mountaineering, camping or boating expeditions, but that is not an argument that is commonly brought or sustained against school expeditions.

On the practical question of arguments for and against co-education, the honest educator has probably to admit that he does not know enough to generalize one way or the other; he holds whichever view he does hold as a matter of belief rather than of experience. But when it comes down to a matter of belief — and here is the real nub of the matter — it becomes clear that the real distinction is not between the supporter of co-education and its opponent, but — and these are by no means the same categories in different words — between the supporter of the traditional sex ethic and its questioner.

The traditional attitude — and again we have to trace a religious origin — of the English and the American towards sex has been that it is something to be ashamed of; the least worthy of the appetites; a rather crude device which man shares with the lower animals; something which men, being more carnal by nature, may be excused for enjoying, but which normal women must just accept. I do not think that this is an unfair travesty of what the vast mass of people in England and in the parts of America where the puritan tradition was very strong were, up to a generation ago, more or less explicitly brought up to feel.

And the interesting thing is that in its reactions against this view the more extreme 'free' school like the 'permissive' adult fringe group will show, by over-emphatic and self-conscious defiance, how much it is still influenced by it. The same influence displays itself in some middle-of-the-road co-educational schools, where a subtle vocabulary of disapprobation, and a rigid system of unwritten law, maintain a segregation between the sexes as emphatic and complete as if each sex lived in conventual or monastic remoteness. This combination of separation combined with contiguity would appear, from either the 'distraction' or the 'fantasy' point of view, to be making the worst of both worlds.

What we are saying in fact is that a genuine, rational, positive and systematic replacement of the old sex ethic by a new has not yet been attempted. Yet this must be as important as anything that the philosophy of progressive education should do. A timidity which of its nature admits the opposing arguments, and equally a defiant and negative reversal of conventional practice and language — *pour épater les bourgeois* — are likely only to arouse such considerable opposition that co-education as an educational principle will not be rationally examined at all.

Most co-educationists reveal in their practice the kind of confusion betrayed in their arguments. Reluctant to admit even to themselves the extent of the break with traditional attitude in which their belief involves them, they lack both courage and conviction, and vacillate between regarding the mixing of the sexes at school as a sort of homeopathic medicine, an inoculation against thinking sex important later, and regarding it as a genuine introduction to the mutual adjustments which a common life between adult men and women entails. Yet either view clearly excludes the other; the first admits the traditional sex ethic as valid, the second rejects it. Those who wish to inoculate adolescents against emotional involvement (frequently and most ineptly termed 'silliness') betray by their language and behaviour the kind of pre-occupation they deplore: they share the traditional moral outlook to a degree often far more hysterically timid than conventional educators. Indeed, it probably does less harm to call adolescent love-making wrong than to call it silly. The former is at least an honest attempt to treat serious things seriously, and not to run away from them. And the adolescent, provided he or she is not frightened, can think of right and wrong in behaviour as a matter for rational consideration and discussion; the charge of silliness is a stab in the back against which there is no defence, or rather against which the only defence is a shell of cynicism or sophistication which may well grow part of the *persona*, and defeat any growth of moral or aesthetic sensibility. The essence of adolescene is instability; children suspect and fear their own inexperience, and they know quite well that they tend to act irrationally and impulsively, arrogantly and humourlessly, because of it. Unsympathetic ridicule is the adult's most devastating weapon, and when, as here, it is used to ward off and mask the adult's own secret misgivings, it is the least defensible.

At the other extreme — and this is by no means unknown in modern co-educational practice either — there is the attitude that is so sympathetic to adolescent emotional problems that it can never leave well alone. It is having to pull the young plant out of the ground all the time to make sure that it is growing properly. It will 'match-make', throw particular children together, encourage them to talk about their feelings and experiences, discuss emotional development with them in psychological terms, and be aggressively frank and forthright about sexual matters. The result tends to be an embarrassed hothouse. Children are far more easily shocked than their own language and behaviour often apparently suggest, and they distinguish far more sharply and accurately than the grown-up between the quality of their own adolescent emotional relationships and what the adult appears to be talking about. On the whole, while they may on occasion seek information or advice, they commonly much prefer to be allowed emotional privacy, and to manage their own affairs in their own way and at their own pace. As we have already suggested, one of the most frequent and most dangerous things that teachers tend to do is to read their own lives into the lives of their pupils, and unconsciously to get a vicarious satisfaction out of the adolescent enjoying an emotional life that they themselves failed to achieve. The children are likely to react either by taking sex as much more a matter of course than it is, or by running away from it. In either case sensitivity is lost.

Thus both these types of modern co-educationist are fundamentally still within the tradition which they overtly criticize. Neither has yet achieved a new or positive ethic about adolescent sex to replace either a rationalized or inverted puritanism. Yet, if we are at all on the right lines, the whole raison d'être of co-education is that it could and should be the kind of introduction to adult life that makes for increasing the sensitivity of each sex towards the other, not diminishing it. Freedom in this context means precisely the same positive and constructive opportunity that we have defined it as meaning in others. Unless co-education does this, as an educational principle it is a failure, and no arguments, whether about naturalness or about the dangers of emotional precocity, have any relevance.

It seems to me that there is a presumption, though not an overwhelming one, in favour of co-education making for more sensitive and more rounded personalities than segregated education. Whether in fact it does so will depend entirely on the general atmosphere of the school; co-education, in itself, can be either a help or a hindrance. If the atmosphere is one in which emotional relationships are either actively discouraged or actively encouraged, then having the two sexes mixed will probably do more harm than good. If on the other hand the atmosphere is one in which children's affections for each other are as normal and unstressed as any other interest, such as bird-watching or swimming or dramatics, which the two sexes may have in common, then co-education can contribute something of the greatest possible value to the growth of an integrated personality in both boy and girl. It is an aspect of individual development to be approved, watched inconspicuously, and not interfered with unnecessarily.

In the last half century, we have been going through a revolution of thought and practice about matters of sex. The older generation is slow to acknowledge this; old taboos, and the old conspiracy of silence about such matters, are still strong. But in both England and the USA – perhaps more manifestly in the USA – the climate of manners and morals has changed very considerably; the puritan tradition, as far as the generation under the age of forty is concerned, has weakened almost to vanishing point. Two world wars have greatly contributed to this; so has the theatre, the cinema, television, and a very great deal more frankness in the visual arts. We may like it or dislike it, but if we are honest we must accept it as a fact. Sex today is of absorbing interest, equally for both sexes. If anyone doubts this, let him watch television advertisements, go regularly to the theatre or the movies, or read the glossier weekly magazines. Whatever we may think or feel about this revolution, we must realize that its greatest impact has been on the adolescent. Teenage friendships and romances are now accepted in a way and to an extent that would have been undreamt of two generations ago; children still of school age enjoy freedoms that would have profoundly shocked their grandfathers and grandmothers. The English and American boy and girl are a great deal more sexually aware than they were fifty years ago — or at least than they would have allowed themselves to appear to be. It is significant that there is in the present generation a strong tendency towards early marriages; late maturity is ceasing to be an accepted feature of our society. There is no longer the powerful taboo that used to exist against physical intimacy before marriage; it has been estimated that in contemporary England at least one girl in four is pregnant before marriage takes place, and that complete physical intimacy is commonplace among older teenagers. Whatever the modern young think wrong — and it is not in the least that they are lacking in moral sense: witness the campaigns for nuclear disarmament and against apartheid — sex as such does not fall into this category, either inside or outside marriage.

All this is very relevant to the subject of co-education, and it reinforces what I said earlier about the unreality of the familiar arguments. Without, so far, very much help from their elders, the young are in process of constructing a new sex ethic for themselves. We have to admit that it is likely to be more honest, and productive of greater happiness, than the sex ethic of semi-obsolete religious tradition. The idea of sex as interesting fun is undoubtedly revolutionary, and to many people undoubtedly shocking. It is an idea which most opponents of co-education resent and suspect, even when it is not present; it is an idea which many if not most co-educationists themselves shrink from, and because of this tend to obscure and travesty the concept of freedom as an educational principle.

The mistake both make is that because an idea is subversive it must also be anarchic. Yet this manifestly need not be true, any more than it was true over the general question of freedom. The duty of adult responsibility remains; the ends for which he is working are clear. But his criteria are not any more, even as concealed assumptions, overtones left behind by a religious ethic in which he no longer believes; they are the happiness and integrity and potentiality of the individual boy and girl. The adult, that is to say, will not impress on the adolescent that chastity is a virtue — because it may or may not be, according to individual circumstances. But he may have to suggest quite plainly at some moment in a fifteen-year-old boy-girl relationship that for a number of specific reasons actual sexual intercourse at that age and stage of development would be unwise, and might do serious damage to both their lives. Normally, such moments will be rare; adolescent children of this age, living and working freely together, do not commonly appear to seek complete sexual expression, though they will indulge in a good deal of exploratory sexual play. At a later stage, when adulthood has really been reached — and it is important to realize that it is today reached much earlier than a generation ago — this kind of rational advice and discouragement may be inadequate and inappropriate, and it may be the adult's duty, in the interests of society, and the boy's and girl's own future welfare, to give them precise information about contraception.

There appear, as in adult life, to be for the adolescent three distinct, if allied, types of sex relationship: the enjoyment of sexual play as such, the realization of romance, and the demand for affectionate companionship, which may or may not be accompanied by physical demonstrativeness. It is part of the adult's role to see that no one of these is either unnecessarily thwarted, or artificially stimulated, and that a balance is kept. As between equals in age and emotional experience, the adult should interfere as little as possible, either to encourage or discourage: the more benevolently passive he is, the more likely he is to receive confidences, and to be able to give profitable counsel. As between unequals, he has to be watchful for signs of exploitation. Neither ruthlessness nor perversity is acceptable in our ethic, and this holds for homosexual as well as for heterosexual relationships. The most difficult decision for the adult is not so much what to do or say, as when: judging the point at which to step in. His only safeguard — and this is true of every school, whether co-educational or not — is the confidence he has managed to inspire. Here, as generally, being matter-of-fact seems to be the best policy; the hearty, the earnest and the over-anxious tend to get left in the dark.

The content of the curriculum has a definite
relevance to the growth of personality and intellectual capacity

We come, lastly, to the question of the curriculum itself.
Two separate questions are involved here: one administrative, the other cultural. Both have ethical implications.
First, it is desirable on our ethical premises that the habits
of work and of concentration should be acquired, that mental
alertness and curiosity should be stimulated and cultivated.
The administrative question is, by what methods can this
best be done? Second, there is the whole question of a
'liberal education', a curriculum planned with a definite
cultural content and direction in the light of the values
earlier laid down. Is this possible, and what purposes should
it be designed to serve?

Now it is clear on both these counts that we are reckoning
to achieve non-academic ends by primarily academic means.
The standards by which we shall eventually judge the effect
of given subjects and methods on a given child's mind and
character are, in the last analysis, moral standards. The fact
that we are necessarily using roundabout means should make
us highly critical; much more critical than schools in general
appear to be about their methods and the content of their
curricula. If education consists in the realization of individual
capacities — the humanist viewpoint which has been implicit
and explicit throughout this book — then both method and
content must be secondary and subject to particular phases
of particular developments. The only generalizations which
we can lay down with any confidence are thus negative rather
than positive: what a school must avoid doing if it is to
escape the fatal facility of uniformity.

It is this that constitutes the real objection to public
competitive examinations in school life; it is not that they are
difficult or onerous or unintelligently carried out — criticism
of this kind seems to me to have been excessive and misdirec-

ted — but that they are of their nature stultifying; they impose teaching techniques and limit the range of school interests at the age of maximum intellectual curiosity, making a spurious cleavage, in the minds of both the schools and the general public, between important and unimportant activities. 'O' and 'A' levels are not bad examinations for the average intelligent child; the range of subjects is very reasonably wide, and standards are not unduly exacting. But for such examinations to determine the entry into almost any career which will bring boys and girls more than a subsistence level of income, and offer them work of more than merely routine character, is a sterile state of affairs, probably worse in its intellectual and social consequences than the most unblushing system of nepotism and patronage.

The character of the means, then, is clear, whether they be those of content or of method; they should be such as to provide that opportunity for continuous initiative which has been defined as freedom. 'An education which does not begin by evoking initiative and end by encouraging it must be wrong. For its whole aim is the production of active wisdom.' So said that greatest of contemporary educational philosophers, Alfred North Whitehead, and we can but echo it whole-heartedly.

Now here again there is frequently a confusion in both the traditional and the modern approaches. The traditionalist still clings to the idea, which contains a half-truth, that the mind can be sharpened and disciplined by particular studies. Both Latin and Geometry have been justified their place in the curriculum on little other ground. It is, in this form, a very dangerous idea, for it implies that the mind is an inert instrument, and by treating it as such tends to make it so. For any subject to have an awakening and disciplining value it must have an intrinsic interest; if that intrinsic interest is there, almost any subject can be made awakening and disciplining. A child who hates Mathematics and likes Contract Bridge will learn more of the virtues of precision, logical deduction and probability theory from Contract Bridge than he will ever learn from Mathematics as a school subject. This is not an argument for including Contract Bridge in the curriculum (though some American schools do so, for reasons that are social rather than intellectual); it is an argument against

teaching Mathematics or any other subject to numbly resist-
ant minds. To quote Professor Whitehead again:

> The mind is never passive; it is a perpetual activity,
> delicate, receptive, responsive to stimulus. You
> cannot postpone its life until you have sharpened it.
> Whatever interest attaches to your subject matter
> must be evoked here and now; whatever powers
> you are strengthening in the pupil. must be exer-
> cised here and now; whatever possibilities of mental
> life your teaching should impart, must be exhibited
> here and now.

But — and here is the half-truth — method is important in
either bringing out or failing to bring out the awakening and
disciplining qualities inherent in any subject. If children are
in fact free to follow out their own interests, then it is the
function of a teaching staff to see that these interests are
pursued consistently and constructively. All activity should
be strenuous. There is a tendency now, I am inclined to think,
in many schools to overstress the 'play' approach to intellectual activity, to make things primarily entertaining. This is a
natural reaction from a traditional approach to teaching that
made dullness a virtue in itself. But while all teaching should
seek to be interesting, high professional standards of subject
matter should prevail in secondary schools at least, and these
standards should not be watered down to capture or maintain
children's interest. In fact children should be discouraged, by
the standard expected, and by the attitude of teachers
towards their own subjects, from taking up subjects in which
they have no inherent interest, but which their parents or
they feel vaguely that they should be doing. Mind-sharpening
and intellectual discipline cannot be automatically acquired
from particular subjects, but they can emphatically be
acquired from teachers who, from their own absorptions and
enthusiasms, exact as a precondition of study an attitude of
serious application in all subjects taken up, from Greek to
Woodwork. One of the very strong arguments in favour of
teachers being given, apart from their teaching load, opportunity and leisure to pursue their own intellectual work, is
that this can create an atmosphere that is catching, and that
from it children can get a sense of dedication to mental

endeavour, a sense that there is an adventure, and not only a routine chore, of learning.

On the question of the content and bias of the curriculum as a whole it is impossible to be categorical. Yet however elastic a good school should be — and it should be very elastic — in order to cater for all legitimate interests, however exceptional, all schools must in practice have their curricula tailored primarily to fit the average range of interest and intelligence. It is permissible, then, to consider, however tentatively and with all due reservations and warnings against rigidity, a normal minimum of subjects to be the intellectual and cultural framework within which the great majority of children would have the best chance to develop along the lines which we have already defined as good.

The main problem and task for very young children is the building up of their own personalities, the realization of their own powers, and the creation of relationships with their fellows. It seems, therefore, on this showing, that the Primary School of today is right in laying especial stress upon both practical and artistic activities, things designed to awaken a child's imagination and sensibility, and also to make him feel physically adequate in tackling the phenomenal and material world which surrounds him. Music, Poetry, Painting, Storytelling and Play-acting, on the one hand, and simple manual skills such as Carpentry, Pottery, Household Repairs, Cookery and Housemaiding on the other, are of first-class importance, first in presenting a wide range of different types of activities and, second, in making all work appear of equal importance, so that children may become aware of the interdependence of work, and may avoid later both the direct snobbishness towards manual work that has happily almost vanished in Western countries but is still deplorably dominant in Eastern, and the equally pernicious inverted moral snobbery, growing in the West, of the anti-intellectual, who all too often arrogates to himself the class-conscious title of 'worker', as if the only work of practical and social importance is done in the pit or on the shop floor.

But if the modern Primary School and Kindergarten are right in making practical and artistic activities the main features of their curriculum, they also tend to be rather undiscriminating about them, and to be uncritical of their effects upon children of the more academic and intellectual type. The jargon of educational psychology has become platitudinous and misleading; the idea of perpetually creating in the classroom a 'life-situation', and of making the content of the curriculum grow from 'a child's own experience', can become in the hands of the doctrinaire and inexpert as sterile as the traditional idea of keeping children with their noses glued to their desks. It is true that many children, for quite a long time, can only learn abstractions like addition and subtraction from practical and physical examples; it is equally true that many children get past that stage very quickly, and get bored and contemptuous at being kept back and offered mental pap instead of the meat they might profitably get their teeth into. And to be intellectually bored is probably even more dangerous to a child's development than to be intellectually pushed.

Further, although the traditional school tended to lay too much stress on the acquisition of elementary skills at an early age, the modern school is often far too casual and unexacting. Reading and Writing and Arithmetic are not of themselves important except in so far as they make other learning and experience possible. But they are important for that reason, and they are much harder to learn later on. The subject matter of their acquisition is necessarily infantile, and the child who has passed beyond Kindergarten stage resents and resists having to go back to it. It seems to me that it is one of the more important functions of a Junior School to bring out the need for these elementary techniques in the development of other interests, to devote definite time to formal work, and to exact definite standards. Unless this is done, there is a real danger, which has become manifest in the USA, and is spreading in this country, of children reaching the age of eleven or twelve, not only illiterate, but, what is even more important, unused and hostile to the idea of systematic work. All this is of moral as well as of intellectual importance. A school atmosphere in which a large number of interesting and stimulating activities are taking place tends to lack repose and consistent application. The formal side of the curriculum should be designed to correct this without sacrificing fundamental interests, and by the formal side I mean not only formal work in reading, writing and other things, but also a certain formality in classroom atmosphere for even the youngest children; casualness, messiness and noise, even if not positively disorderly, are time and energy-wasting and educationally unproductive.

Similarly, modern Primary School and Kindergarten teachers are often far too doctrinaire and undiscriminating about the value of letting children follow up their own interests and organize their own time. For the absence of adult organization does not necessarily have the admirable results that these slogans would appear to suggest. What may very easily happen, especially if the teacher is himself or herself reacting against a narrowly academic bias in the past, is the creation in the school of an anti-intellectualist atmosphere in which the children are subtly and unconsciously discouraged from intellectual interests and from the development of any consistent intellectual application. Children are explicitly encouraged to paint and model and keep pets, to go riding and do gardening and farmwork and spend a great deal of time out of doors; and if they are sufficiently absorbed and occupied by all these to shirk the comparative tedium of learning to read and write or any other formal work, the teacher is not on the whole disapproving; in fact he or she is commonly more approving of these children than of those who would like to be left alone with a book.

In such an atmosphere, many children can go on for years without acquiring the most elementary skills; they get into a convention that reading or writing or arithmetic is something they don't, can't and needn't do, and when the time comes that these things can be postponed no longer, the effect on the child is one of acute inferiority and discouragement that he should now find so hard what others of his age can do so easily. Further, to let a group of children be largely its own judge of how it spends its time is to put the decision into the hands of the strongest and most extrovert elements; it can be to impose on the less tough or more intellectually minded individual a régime far more sterile and tyrannical than that of the trained adult.

There is great and justified concern, both in England and in the USA, about the teaching of English. Standards of accuracy in the use of language, as well as the perhaps less important standards of handwriting and spelling, have certainly declined considerably, and a great deal of this decline must be put down to lack of time and attention given to English at Primary School level. Yet to learn the correct use of one's own native tongue must surely be cardinal to all other kinds of learning; precision and grace of expression are fundamental to comprehension and communication both in the sciences and in the arts. Hence children from the earliest possible age should start by being read to, and then be encouraged to read and write for themselves; they should also be encouraged — and they do not need very much encouragement — to learn by heart; this can lead to the unconscious acquisition of an ear for style in writing, as well as to an increasing mental storehouse of vocabulary and phrase. On this point I am unrepentantly old-fashioned. Some attention should be given, increasing as the child's competence increases, to handwriting and spelling; enough to discourage sloppiness, not so much as to discourage freedom of expression and inventiveness. Overmuch attention to formal grammar in English, or indeed in any living language, tends to defeat its own ends; the teaching of a living language should be functional. One argument in favour of retaining Latin or Greek in the school curriculum, and starting with it fairly early, is that the structure of language can be learnt very much more easily through either of these, and structure once learnt is useful for any language. It can be treated as a formal game, and most children enjoy formal games.

I should like to see at least one modern language taught to young children not as an isolated timetable subject, but as they would have it presented to them in a much more drastic and wholesale way if they went abroad. There has been in recent years an enormous advance in the functional teaching of French; there is an increasing tendency to present the language through visual and 'real life' situations, and this process could be carried much further. This presents administrative difficulties, but they are not insuperable and I have seen them overcome; they are a slight price to pay for making French what it certainly is not in many if not most English schools, a language which actual people actually use.

Elementary General Science should certainly be taught in Junior Schools, and this should include a lot of practical and experimental work of a simple kind; accuracy in manipulation can hardly be learnt too early. There is little need, in most modern schools, to stress the importance of Nature Study; that, with elementary Biology and Hygiene, is normally well taken care of. It is manifestly important to give the growing child an increasing awareness of the world around him and an understanding of the way his own body works.

Geography, in the sense of how big the world is, what makes night and day, where places are, who lives where and how — all this is extremely suitable for a Junior School. Further, with the use of television, films, filmstrips and other teaching aids, it can all be made extremely graphic; the world and its peoples can be brought into the classroom. Such presentation is not only interesting in itself; it brings in a host of other subjects, such as transport, clothes, climate, food and customs, which widen imaginative experience as well as factual knowledge of the external world. It is customary these days to attach great importance to practical local or 'environmental' studies; when these are well done and integrated with other work this importance can be justified. But this is not invariably so, and such studies are often not nearly as closely related to 'the child's own experience' as teachers would like to think. There is a limit to the value to be got out of expeditions to local shops and industries, and to the construction of plasticine maps.

History, as commonly taught in Junior Schools — and, indeed, in many Senior Schools as well — is mainly, as Henry Ford suggested, bunk. Most that is of value to the younger child can be better presented as story or legend, and such stories and legends should be drawn from many countries and peoples over a wide range of the past. Again, many primary school teachers are obsessed with the idea that the very difficult subject of pre-history is especially related to the young child's world of comprehension and experience; apart from teaching a great deal of extremely dubious history, there is little to make such material come to life. Social history, such as the History of Transport, Communications, Writing and the Alphabet, Costume and the like, is far more illuminating, and far more nearly related to the child's interests.

The change from a Primary to a Secondary School should mark a real stage in development. The phase of imaginative adventuring and of social adjustments is mainly over; the

next phase should be that of developing interests now discovered, and of widening social relationships to include more
than the immediate contemporary group. This is the phase in
which real intellectual effort is about to become possible, if it
is going to become possible at all, the phase in which phenomena need to be both studied and interpreted, and rational
generalizations about them made. Lastly, it is the phase in
which the individual should be able to evolve out of his
interests and his pursuit of them a sense of style, that intangible personal sense of standards which distinguishes the
serious worker from the dabbler, the sense of economy, fit-
ness and shapeliness that is integral to the creative process.

For these reasons, I should like to see, for the twelve to
sixteen age range, a Senior School curriculum built around
two main themes. One would be a unified and coherent Social
Science Course, which would include, as separate but related
subjects, Modern History, both Western and Eastern, Geography, both world and regional, some Government and
Political Science, and some elementary Economics; this
would be a four-year course, the scope and purpose of which
would be to interpret to the adolescent boy and girl the social
and international world which he and she are entering. The
second would be an analogous course in the physical and
biological sciences, which would again include as separate but
related subjects Physics, Chemistry, Biology, Bio-chemistry,
Zoology, Anatomy and Geology, to present the natural world
as an intelligible whole. Both these courses would necessarily
be elastic, and subject to continual criticism and revision, but
they should be clear in aim, stringent in method, and their
intellectual content should be such as to encourage and make
possible later specialization for the boy or girl who is going
on to University work or its equivalent after two or three
further years at school.

Supplementary to these should be a wide choice. Latin or
Greek should be kept up only by those who have become
interested in them for their own sakes; Mathematics, after
a two-year general course which would give the non-specialist
all he needs for life, should be continued only as a specialist
subject by those who have that bent or need. I am intention-
ally neglecting here examination requirements as being irrelevant in a discussion of fundamental educational aims; never-

theless, it would be perfectly possible to reconcile such a curriculum with existing GCE or Matriculation standards. Astronomy, Logic and Philosophy should be possible extensions of interest for older children with a bent for scientific or formal studies; Anthropology, Comparative Religion and Ancient or Medieval History for those with sociological interests. In each instance the standards set, even at quite an early stage, should be professional, not dilettante.

At least one modern language should be taken; to become reasonably at home in two world languages besides one's own might fairly be regarded as one of the norms of a liberal education. In a Secondary School the study should naturally be more formal than in a Primary, but it should be backed up by trips abroad and school exchange visits for, if possible, a term at a time. The teaching of English language should be continued for the first two years, after which time, if the Junior School has done its work properly, it should become unnecessary as a separate subject. English Literature should be optional, but children should be encouraged by library facilities and by adult advice and discussion to read widely and to talk critically about what they read. Music and the visual arts — which now include television and cinema — should be capable of serious study, and should rank in curriculum importance as high as any literary or scientific subject. And for the child with only very limited academic interests there should be a wide range of practical arts and sciences available. While vocational education as such is not desirable at school age, skills such as carpentry, furniture-making, boat-building, metal-work, the elements of mechanical and electrical engineering, plumbing, building and building design, agriculture and animal husbandry, gardening, cookery and housekeeping, nursing, first aid and child care — all of these, without occupational differentiation between the sexes, are valuable extensions of experience which can afford a basis for later choice of career.

History teaching at the Secondary level is now generally very much better and more intelligently done than it used to be; it is no longer solely political history, and the better textbooks in common use attempt to give the pupil something of a general picture — often with authentic documentary and visual source-material — of the social and economic life of the time. But such attempts remain peripheral; examination syllabuses and teaching time are still largely conditioned by the reigns of monarchs, the tergiversations of politicians, and the conduct of wars.

Yet if the study of history is to be at all profitable and meaningful at this stage, it must surely be wider in scope, more integrated in content, and more comprehensibly related to the complex of contemporary life into which the pupil is being inducted. History should not be compartmented, any more than life is, into 'political', 'economic', 'social' and suchlike categorizations. A sense of the reality of the lives, motives and institutions of people living in time and place other than one's own is not an easy thing to acquire; history is on the whole a rather adult study. But history teaching in school can do much more than is commonly done to give a sense of period, by weaving together the difficult strands of an age into a coherent fabric, which the pupil can recognize as comparable with, if very different from, the fabric of life around him. Thus, rather than the wild gallop over the surface of the centuries which English text-books, and American more so, commonly give, it would seem to me preferable to have an intensive study of a series of rather short historical periods, and attempt over these small areas to delineate and correlate a number of humanly related aspects. It is seldom, for instance, that even an enlightened teacher tries to bring into the period which he is teaching the achievements and peculiar idiom of the age in art, music, literature and scientific development. But it surely would be illuminating, to take only one example, for a boy or girl to realize that, during the reigns of the later Stuarts in England and Louis XIV in France, Vermeer and Lely were painting their pictures; Wren was building St Paul's Cathedral and Le Nôtre the Palace of Versailles; Purcell, Bach and Handel were composing their music; Dryden and Racine were writing poetry and plays, while in the newly created Royal Society Newton, Boyle and others were laying the foundations of modern science and technology. One could multiply such congruences almost indefinitely, but the point is that all these things were as much part of the ambience of the age that I have instanced as television, pop-music, Picasso, Le Corbusier, paperbacks and space-travel are of our own. Nor, without this kind of background, will visits to museums or picture galleries, or romps through anthologies, contribute very much that is meaningful to a child's understanding.

Again, from another angle, dates need not be the meaningless bugbear that they have acquired the reputation of being. It may be illuminating in developing a sense of historical causation and continuity to point, for example, to the year 1642 as that in which Galileo died and Newton was born, or to the year 1867, in which occurred the invention of dynamite, the publication of Marx's *Das Kapital*, and the enfranchisement of the urban proletariat in England. Used in such a way, in discussing the development of an age, dates can assume an exciting significance ordinarily denied to them. All this is to ask a great deal of both teachers and their pupils; it is also to put forward the now somewhat revolutionary idea that to create a literate and liberally educated society, a literate and liberally educated teaching profession has first — and yet — to be created.

To sum up. It is, I have suggested, a justifiable charge against both the progressive and the conventional school that neither has developed the theory and practice of either academic or non-academic education much beyond the levels bequeathed by their predecessors. There have been a number of advances, some set-backs, but little or no new thinking. There are more — and some better — opportunities for more children to do more things, but that is about all. The greater part of the responsibility for this static and somewhat complacent state of education must lie with the progressive school, whose principal *raison d'être* has been its claim to forward-mindedness. On the question of what constitutes a 'liberal education'; on the extent to which the academically minded can or should share a curriculum with the non-academically minded; on the even more difficult question of whether or not — or to what extent and at what age — children should be separated into streams based on assessed IQ and attainment level rather than on chronological age or social compatibility; on the validity of such assessments and by whom they should be made — on these and many allied points the theory and practice of the modern school is not nearly as explicit or enlightening as one could wish. There are many other neglected questions of contemporary practical importance: should school buildings, classroom design and timetable construction be more elastic? What is the value of drama work in school? Do specific crafts have measurable psychological or therapeutic effect? Can competition as a stimulus to achievement in either work or play be eliminated, and is it desirable that it should be? What other forms of motivation can be substituted? What subjects, if any, should be regarded as compulsory, and what optional? Should the latter be taken up and dropped at will, or should there be a minimum trial period? What degree of importance should be attached to external examination requirements, and what degree of pressure is it permissible for a school to put on pupils to meet these, in the considered interest of the individual's own future in contemporary society? Above all, what should be the content and structure of a curriculum designed for the world of tomorrow? It is clear that these are some of the numerous legitimate — even urgent — lines of enquiry and research, which should be capable of at least tentative and provisional answers in the light of the actual experience of schools which are professedly experimental.

The foregoing chapter — indeed, the whole of this study — was written from the standpoint of a traditional liberal humanist, and it would be disingenuous to pretend that the writer is anything else. But it is only fair to point out that at the present time the whole concept of traditional liberal education is in question; a new dimension in educational thinking is beginning to take shape. The present social matrix, of which the educational system is one not very successful aspect, is clearly in process of change — change far more radical than such facile and unrewarding panaceas as raising the school-leaving age or creating more and bigger colleges and universities. Traditional formal curricula — the common core of subjects supposed by our grandfathers to be the fortifying discipline of school for adult life — are being increasingly challenged; we are now looking to produce not so much good students as versatile individuals capable of participating in society. The school can no longer be regarded as a closed box into which children are put at the age of five, and from which they are released on school-leaving, supposedly equipped for some activity profitable to themselves and to the community. Educational boundaries generally have become far more elastic, both inside and outside the classroom. This can be evidenced in school architecture as well as in school content, and in the growing demand for pupil participation in school administration. The influences of radio and television, of local environmental studies involving the whole community, of school interchange visits both at home and abroad — these have been and are of immense importance. In higher education the advent of the Open University has probably been the most significant phenomenon of our time, and has both directly and indirectly narrowed the gap between school and adult life.

What we seem in fact to be doing is shifting the emphasis from teaching to learning, and learning is coming to be regarded very much more as an integral part of life rather than as an introduction to it. The school is becoming less divorced from its social context, and there is increasing awareness of the need to develop the ability and the desire for continuing self-instruction. It has been established that children — even quite small children — can show marked talents for organizing their own learning activities. In this connection I recall a salutary incident from my own first term as a teacher. A small boy who had been persistently missing classes was rebuked for wasting time. His response was unanswerable: 'I'm not *wasting* time; I'm *spending* time.'

In other words, we may be beginning to take a quite revolutionary new 'consumer' approach to education; if school does not offer the pupil what he needs — and the contemporary Secondary School system patently often does not — he feels entirely justified in shopping elsewhere. Looked at in this way, social problems of truancy and the like can perhaps be seen more as the system's failure than the pupil's fault: school has ceased to hold anything meaningful for him. This 'consumer approach' cannot be disregarded; the teacher's role must be from now on to structure the educational programme in terms of the student's skills, capacities and inclinations, rather than in terms of subject material. As I said earlier, this is to ask of teachers — and of teacher-training colleges — a great deal more than we are now doing.

With all this, and acknowledging much of its validity, we have to be realistic. We cannot run before we can walk, and while we are still so shaky as a society on even the fundamentals of literacy and numeracy, we are still only stumbling towards any radical reform. We therefore cannot throw out formal class teaching and curricula incontinently, and while drastic experiments with 'de-schooling' are often very successful with the more than averagely intelligent pupils and more than averagely dedicated and competent staff, the lack of a basic framework of hours, curricula and text-books causes the average and below-average pupil and teacher alike to feel rudderless and insecure, and lacking the confidence given by the achievement of even a minor goal both tend to drift into apathy.

Moreover, all over the world pressures of sheer numbers and of political egalitarianism have enforced massive standardization, and this militates strongly against the kind of elasticity that I have been discussing. To a large extent we have become victims of our own educational systems; the inevitable institutionalization of education has brought on a near paralysis of growth. Also, we must realize that we may, by abandoning the older conventional restraints of the classroom and by giving unremitting freedom of choice, impose far too great a psychological strain upon developing personalities. We cannot altogether ignore two facets of contemporary life which are basically symptoms of personal insecurity: an irrational cult of violence in almost every field — political demonstration, industrial action, sport, television, the cinema, the theatre and the arts generally — and an equally irrational retreat into pseudo-religions and other forms of drugs. Both these have very dangerous implications for the coherence of our society.

All these considerations should give us pause before we talk too confidently about new dimensions in education. What I wrote in the last chapter about the concept of a liberal education may well have become irrelevant in twenty years' time, but it is not so yet. While we are right to look towards a possible glimmer at the end of the educational tunnel, we must realize that we have still a long way to grope.

In summary, certain of the points we have been making are perhaps worth underlining. The traditional emphasis of all education in England has been and remains on the development of character rather than of knowledge. The modernist school has accepted unquestioningly this characteristic, and has carried it even further than the conventional. More or less openly the Public Schools and the Grammar Schools have said, with the full approval of their parental market — 'We don't mind what a boy learns at school if he learns to be a gentleman.' And for girls, although there is no precise equivalent in the language, the ideal and objective is the same. The progressive school says, 'We don't mind what a child learns at school if he or she turns out a happy and well-adjusted individual.' Hence, on some rather ill-considered psychological assumptions, the conventional school continues to stress Games and a broadly humanistic curriculum and repeats, with perhaps a quarter of the tongue in the cheek, the slogans of 'playing the game' and 'the heritage of Greece and Rome'. Equally, on scarcely more considered assumptions, the progressive school stresses Arts and Crafts and Social Science, and repeats the slogans of the teacher-training college about child-centred activities, life-adjustment and children learning by experience with all the simple faith of the Victorian determinist. Both, in the upper ranges of the Secondary School, have been compelled to adapt themselves considerably to the increasingly exigent demands of an age of science and technology, but it is not too harsh to say that they have done so tardily and grudgingly, with the result that the United Kingdom has been in danger of lagging behind a number of other countries in the general level of its educational products. Questions of analysis into educational terms used; of weight, proportion and balance in a curriculum; of the relation of a school régime either to the world as it is or to it as it is likely to be a generation hence; in effect, a sceptical attitude of mind towards the most important of the social sciences − all this is as remarkable by its absence in the progressive school philosophy as it is in the orthodox.

It appears to me that the correspondence between the two poles is more conspicuous than the difference. Even the inconsistencies are striking in their analogous perversity. The orthodox school emphasizes the use of force as a technique and the use of competition as a motive in education, although neither forcefulness nor competitiveness is a particularly gentlemanly characteristic. The modernist school deliberately turns its back on force and competition, without examining the reasonable presumption that either of these might have its place in the development of individuality and initiative. Both types of school tend to be indifferent to the teaching of modern languages, and, with some honourable exceptions, teach them with a laborious and faintly contemptuous inefficacy that finds a tragi-comic correlation in national foreign policy. Yet for children to be at home in languages other than their own should surely rank high in desirability equally with the kind of education that claims to produce leaders in public life and with the kind of education that desires to produce well-adjusted and internationally minded citizens.

The point that I am making is simply this, that the modernist has followed the traditionalist in the kind of attributes he takes to be the aims of education; that he is equally insular, and that where he differs it is as much from reaction as from reasoned conviction. In the past, games have been over-emphasized, and excessive prestige awarded to prowess in them. The arts and manual crafts have been neglected in favour of mainly literary pursuits. Marks and competitive examinations have been a bugbear, setting a dead-end to the development of interests and stultifying initiative. Therefore, the modernist simply turns the tables; prowess at games and formal classroom work are discounted; practical activities and 'self-expression' are at a premium. In neither the intellectual nor the moral field of education is there much that is new, positive or substantial; since Dewey set the pattern of modern education nearly a century ago few original or fundamental questions have been asked about aims, possibilities or techniques. What, in other words, progressive education has been mainly doing — and this is not in the least to under-estimate the necessity and value of the work — is clearing away dead wood; there is little evidence of new planting.

These, then, are the charges that a by no means hostile critic could make against modern so-called 'progressive' education as it now exists both in Great Britain and in the USA; it is, to some extent at least, confused in its premises, negative in its outlook, uncritical in its practice. They are substantial criticisms, and they are worth making for the very reason that this type of education is, on balance, overwhelmingly on the right lines.

Inherent throughout this study has been the theme that it is the individual and his or her development that count. On this, the progressive school is clear: freedom is the means of grace, and individual integrity is the hope of progress. The traditional and conventional school, to the extent that it still remains — and the last half-century has seen radical change — is dominated by the mortmain of a religious ethic that has lost its substance; type-ridden and class-conscious, it belongs to a dying world. It is more important that children's freedoms should be respected excessively and for confused reasons than that they should be over-ridden for no justifiable reasons at all. An education which makes force taboo and sex not taboo at school is, after all, a beacon of light in a world which takes violence for granted, and has resigned itself to unsatisfactory or perverted sexual life as a commonplace. That progressive schools, in the third generation of their existence, should still be leaning over backwards to avoid the dangers of a traditionalism that remains entrenched and powerful in many homes and schools, is evidence of how needed many of their negations were and still are. Punishments *should* be avoided as far as possible; competitiveness *is* undesirable as a dominating motive; corporate loyalty *is*, as often as not, loyalty to a false ideal; good manners, and deference to the feelings of others are desirable emollients in social life, but they are not of prime importance.

All this is not to go back on what has been written earlier; I am suggesting that there are defects which rather more clarity of thought and rather less timidity of practice would go far to remedy, and I am also suggesting that progressive education will become increasingly weaker and more vulnerable unless they are remedied. But it is to restore things to their proper proportion; in its entire purpose and emphasis the progressive school is in accord with the principles which we started by laying down, and the authoritarian school is not.

One final point. Every teacher will and should be able to pick holes in every one of the suggestions and comments I have made. He will point out, quite rightly, that the polarity between the two types of educational outlook which I have been discussing is in practice unreal; that there is an infinite gradation between the two, and that each is learning from the other all the time. He will point out how, for him, the ends — which he may or may not accept as ends — may be, indeed are being, achieved by alternative means. And he will be, for him, perfectly right. But the underlying principles remain. If the approach which this study has developed is anything like a correct one, it is fundamentally attitudes, rather than particular practices, which are important. It is the function and obligation of the teacher to help in developing minds which may in fact be more creative than his own. If he is to do this, and bring out that potential creativeness, he has to be conscious, in the last analysis, of both himself and his pupils as moral beings, and he has to do this without becoming moralistic. Lacking neither self-confidence nor

self-criticism himself, he has to encourage both these qualities in the children with whom he comes in contact. And the
end for which he is working, in them as in himself, is that
constructive sensitivity which is at one and the same time
both Virtue and Intelligence.